T0150831

SUCCESS IS
YOUR OWN
DAMN FAULT!

TITLES BY LARRY WINGET

Get Out of Your Own Way!

Success is Your Own Damn Fault!

The Politically Incorrect Success System

SUCCESS IS YOUR OWN DAMN FAULT!

LARRY WINGET

MEDIA

MEDIA
Published 2020 by Gildan Media LLC
aka G&D Media
www.GandDmedia.com

SUCCESS IS YOUR OWN DAMN FAULT! Copyright © 2020 G&D Media. All rights reserved.

No part of this book may be used, reproduced or transmitted in any manner whatsoever, by any means (electronic, photocopying, recording, or otherwise), without the prior written permission of the author, except in the case of brief quotations embodied in critical articles and reviews. No liability is assumed with respect to the use of the information contained within. Although every precaution has been taken, the author and publisher assume no liability for errors or omissions. Neither is any liability assumed for damages resulting from the use of the information contained herein.

Front cover design by David Rheinhardt of Pyrographx

Interior design by Meghan Day Healey of Story Horse, LLC

Library of Congress Cataloging-in-Publication Data is available upon request

ISBN: 978-1-7225-0229-4

10   9   8   7   6   5   4   3   2   1

Contents

Foreword

Are you ready for a new approach to getting results? Are you ready to get rid of all the old adages, clichés, the seven steps to this, and the twenty-nine secrets to that? Are you ready to be shocked out of the old way of doing things into a new way that's helped people get focused and achieve results in all areas of life?

Number one best-selling author Larry Winget reveals the only thing you need to know to succeed in business and life, and it's this. Ready? *Your success is your own fault.*

Some authors on achievement and motivation stroke your ego by presenting you with information you've already known for years. Others give you detailed statistical analysis of the economy or buy-

ing trends, getting you lost in the pages of boredom
until you have no idea what the book is even about.
Some exploit the hottest buzzword and beat it to
death without giving you any real idea how to do
what they recommend. Or even worse, they tell cute
little parables with inane dialogues and messages so
simple and trite that they are insulting.

As you will quickly learn, these are not Larry's
style. In this refreshingly blunt book, he tells the
unvarnished truth about what it really takes to be
successful. It's *work*.

Are you frustrated with a lack of results at work?
Have you hit a wall? Are you uninspired, stuck in
a rut, feeling underappreciated? Good news. Your
success is not up to your boss, your manager, your
employees, or the economy. It's up to you. Period.
Business is never bad. People are just bad at business, and that flows into all other areas of life as
well.

If that ruffles your feathers, good. This is the
book for you. Larry Winget hacks through the bad
advice given in most success and business books.
He explains why teamwork doesn't work, how we
are all stealing from our companies and ourselves,
that success is simple, and that results are every-

thing. You can forget about thinking outside the box. You're not in a box.

Larry will give you an action plan that can take you from the brink of financial disaster to becoming not merely comfortable—Larry wouldn't have it that way—but rich. You'll be surprised, you will laugh, and you will discover motivation deep down that you never knew you had. Let Larry Winget shock you out of your comfort zone into a whole new league.

Reading this book, you are now completely in charge of your life. You are out of excuses. Does that sound scary?

1

The Most Important Thing

believe that ultimately you want financial security.

To get it, you have to do some things differently.

Remember this: in order to have what you've never had and get something you have never gotten; you have to do something you've never done, which means you're going to have to change the way you live.

You need to say, "I'm better than this. I deserve better than this. I want more than I have right now." You need to look yourself in the eye, slap yourself in the face, and say, "I know I can do better." You need to be your own best friend, kick your own butt, and refuse to tolerate anything except the best from yourself. That's how you get ahead.

From Comfort to Discomfort

Most people live in a very comfortable place. They like it to feel really safe. That's not my style. I'm not a safe person. I don't approach things the way most people do. And my goal is certainly not to make you feel safe. My goal is to make you think about things differently than you've ever thought about things before. I can promise you that in this book I'm going to shock you and hopefully, I'm going to wake you up. I might even tick you off and make you a little bit mad. Good. That's what I want to do. I want you to get out of your comfort zone. I believe people change when they've been made uncomfortable.

Let me give you an example: As you're reading this book, you're probably sitting down. You're going to sit exactly the way you're sitting at this moment until you become uncomfortable. As soon as you become uncomfortable, you shift, move, and change in order to become a bit more comfortable. I want to make you uncomfortable so that you will shift, move, and change in order to go to a better place.

You see, I don't believe we ever make a change in our lives, either personally or professionally, until we've first been made uncomfortable. My goal is to make you uncomfortable. Make you think. Shock you. Wake you up. Make you a little bit mad.

You want to go from where you are to a better place. I think that's what everybody wants. The goal of this book is to help you get from where you are to a better place

At this point you may be saying, "Is this book really for me?" Let me tell you what. If you've ever had a job, if you've ever worked for anyone, if you ever intend to have a job, if you have employees, if you are an employee, if you have a family, if you have a life, if you have a heartbeat, this book is for you, because its goal is to take every single area of your life, from your career to your personal life to your health—right down to how much money you have in your wallet this minute—and make it all just a little bit better.

My intent is to make every area of your life better. Know this: you have to be willing to get better. That's up to you; it's not up to me. I'm fine. I'm in good shape. It's you that I'm concerned about.

I want you to get better, and I know you can. Everybody can get better if they're willing to. You know the old expression: *ready, willing, and able*. I believe everybody is *ready* to be more successful and have a better life. I believe everybody is *able* to get better and have a more successful life. It always comes down to willingness. A lot of people are ready and able, but they're not willing to do what it takes. You have to ask yourself right now: am I willing to do what it takes in order to have a better life? If you are, then read on.

I am going to be offering up some very simple suggestions. This is not complicated stuff, I promise you, and I won't ask you to do anything that I have not personally done myself. I've been where you are. Regardless of where you are, I've been there. I don't care how broke you are. I've been more broke, I promise you.

I don't care about the mistakes that you're experiencing right now. I guarantee you I've made bigger mistakes. I could be the poster child for stupidity in business and life. I've made every mistake you can possibly make. The key is, I learned from those mistakes.

In the last 25 years, I've read four thousand books on success. I've listened to five thousand hours of audio. I've watched that many hours of video from some of the best minds, speakers, authors, trainers that have ever lived, and I learned some things along the way.

I speak from a depth of knowledge, research, and experience. That's what I want to warn you about.

When you listen to someone, ask yourself, "What are they speaking from?" Experience? That's good. Are they speaking from a depth of knowledge? That's always good. Have they researched their topic? That's always good.

I've found that a lot of people are out there speaking and writing books without a clue to what they're talking about. After reading four thousand books that cover thousands of years of information, I've discovered there are really only a handful of good ideas about success. It's not that hard, but it's not what they would lead you to believe.

No Secrets to Success

People are telling you there are secrets to success. I don't believe there are. People are telling you to just cross your fingers and hope for the best. Well, let me tell you right now that a good, positive attitude, crossing your fingers, and hoping for the best is not going to get you anyplace. It takes more.

I can promise you that hope is not a wealth strategy. Wishful thinking is not a strategy for success. It comes down to one thing and one thing only: *work*. You can hope things are going to get better. You can wish things are going to get better. You can have the best attitude in the world. Until you get off your butt and go to work, things are never going to get better for you.

This book is about work. You have to be willing to work. If you're not, you might just as well shut this book right now, because it's not going to do you any good. However, if you are willing to do what it takes, get off your butt, challenge yourself, look yourself in the eye, say, "My situation is my fault, and I created it," and go to work on your situation, I promise you that things will get better for you. That's what you really want: a better life.

You might be saying, "But, Larry, I don't have a traditional job. I don't work nine to five. I work for myself. I own my own company." This book is still perfect for you. I'm going to teach you how to sell more. I'm going to teach you how to deliver better customer service. I'm going to talk to you about ways of managing your people better. I'm going to show you the key to success, which is personal responsibility, and how it applies to you.

I'm going to talk to you about money, how to manage it, how to get more of it, how to use what you have. Everything that I talk about works for everyone in every situation. This book is for you regardless of where you are in your life, because

I've discovered that the principles of success apply to everyone in every situation. What it takes to be a better parent is exactly the same thing it takes to be a better manager or leader or salesperson or entrepreneur.

The Simplicity of Success

It doesn't matter what your goal is; the steps are always the same. Success is very simple. It's not complicated. It's not made up of secrets. I don't use one set of thinking to become a better salesperson and another to become a better leader. The real keys to success are principles that you build your life on, and those principles will work for anyone regardless of their goal.

You can probably tell right now that this book is going to be a little different, and it's going to be very opinionated. You're probably saying, "Why should I read this book by this obnoxious, abrasive, caustic, opinionated guy?"

Let me tell you why: I know what I'm talking about. The stuff I talk about works. I grew up broke. My folks didn't have very much, so when I grew up, I didn't have a whole lot to work with. I worked hard, I watched my parents work hard, and I learned that it takes more than hard work to succeed. I'm going to tell you about what it takes in terms of hard work and what you have to do in addition to hard work.

I worked hard. I went to college, got out of college, and went to work for the telephone company. I was one of the very first male telephone operators in the Bell system. After many years with the Bell system, I left as an area sales manager for AT&T for the state of Kansas. I was an award-winning salesperson for AT&T, and I was a top-ranked sales manager.

I left after divestiture (when the Bell system broke up in the 1980s), started my own telecommunications company, and did very well. One day I went to work as a rich guy. That afternoon I went home absolutely turned upside down and broke. Through a series of mistakes, I lost everything. Believe me, when you're at the bottom, the only thing you can do is go to work, and that's what I did.

That's when I started reading. That's when I started my study of success, and after reading those four thousand books and listening to all those audiotapes and watching all those videos, I discovered what it really takes to be successful.

At that point, I realized that really all in my life I'd ever wanted was an audience. So, I became a professional speaker. I'd started out as a sales trainer as that had been my area of expertise at AT&T and for the Bell system. I quickly discovered that people thought I was funny. Then I found out that they pay you a lot more to make people laugh than they do to teach them how to sell.

Along the way, as a humorist, sales trainer, and funny-guy motivational speaker, I got fed up with what I was saying. I got fed up with what the audience wanted me to say, and I decided I was going to say what I really believed, and what I really believe is this: life is always your own damn fault. It's up to you.

Through your thoughts, words, and actions, you made the mistakes that have created the life you have. If you don't like it, keep it to yourself and go to work on it. Don't whine to the rest of us; we have our own problems.

That's when I really hit a nerve with my audience and became very popular. And that's when I started being honest with myself, saying what I really believed, and saying what I thought the audience really needed to hear instead of what they wanted to hear.

You're going to discover that you're not going to want to learn some of what I have to say in this book, but you probably are going to understand very quickly that you need to learn it. If it strikes a nerve, if it makes you uncomfortable, if it makes you mad, it's probably something you need to hear. That's a lesson I learned along the way. The things I didn't like to hear, the things that upset me the most, were the things that I actually needed to hear the most.

As a result, I've spoken to nearly four hundred Fortune 500 companies. I have written several best-selling books. I have traveled around the world and speak to all kinds of business organizations and associations. I'm a member of the Speaker Hall of Fame. I have had my own television show on A&E where I talked to people who have made financial disasters of their lives. I am a regular on many national television shows on the topics of personal finance, parenting and business.

I'm not a professor of economics, and I don't have a PhD in business. All I have is many years of street experience, and I have a lot of research under my belt. I speak from a depth of knowledge and experience, and I promise you, I'm writing from my heart and from my gut. This is stuff that I know works. I can promise you it will work, whether you're a white-collar, blue-collar, or no-collar employee. I have information that can get you to a better place.

How Hard You Really Work

You probably love telling your friends how hard you worked today or how tired you were when you came home from work. Let me tell you how much you really work. If you're an average person, you don't work very much. That bothers you, doesn't it? But it's the truth. Most people just don't work nearly as much as they tell themselves and others they do. One study I read said that 100 percent of people only work half the time they're at work. If this study is correct, it takes twice as many people as necessary to actually get the job done. Do you know what that translates to? Higher costs, higher insurance costs, higher employee costs, higher taxes; it means that the end product costs more. It costs us when people don't work, and that's the key.

People aren't working. They think when they go to work, they have the right to do what they want, and they don't have to work very hard doing what their employer wants. That's not the way it works. You are being paid to do what your employer hired you to do. That's the deal you made.

You've heard this before: a deal is a deal. When you went to work for your company, you made a deal that you would provide a certain amount of work and they would pay you a certain amount of money. I'm betting they're still showing up with the money. I'm also betting you're not showing up with that amount of work.

My dad worked for Sears, Roebuck for forty-seven years. That's seventeen thousand days. He went to work for Sears when he was seventeen, got two years off to fight World War II, and worked there for a total of forty-seven years.

Every single day, he worked with, for, and around idiots. (So, do you, don't you? Look around. I mean, be honest. Of course, you do.) Every single day, he had customers who were idiots. A lot of those seventeen thousand days, he didn't feel good, he didn't have much motivation or a good attitude. He had problems, but he still did his job every day. Why?

My father made a deal, and the deal was that he would work. That's what he was hired to do. It was a deal based on commitment. I think that's what's lacking today. We've lost that commitment. We forget that we gave our word and that our word was to do what we were hired to do.

"They're not giving me my fifteen minutes' break." Sure they are. You took your fifteen minutes when you were dilly-dallying on the computer or on your phone surfing the Internet on time that your company was paying you for. That's not right. In fact, that's stealing.

At the end of the day, look back at everything that you've done and ask, "Was I paid to do those things? Was that in my agreement? Did I say I would do those things? Did they pay me to do those things?" Chances are that you did a lot of things that they didn't pay you for, that weren't a part of your deal. In other words, you weren't working. That's the key. That bothers me.

You were hired to work. You were hired to be productive. You were hired to get results. That's why they hired you. You were there to generate more revenue for the company than you actually cost. Your contribution has to outweigh your expense.

So look at what you do every single day. Do you contribute more than you cost? If you don't, then you aren't needed. They ought to fire you and find someone who does contribute at least what they cost.

Think about if you owned the company (and maybe you do own the company). Look at your employees. Don't you want them to bring more to the table than they cost? If they don't, there's no way to be profitable. Sometimes we forget that we are there to contribute to the overall profitability of the organization that pays our salary. We don't always do that.

Productivity sucks, and the reason it sucks, the reason you get bad service, the reason things cost so much, the reason it's hard to walk in a retail store and find somebody to take your money or wait on you or answer a question, the reason you call someone and the phone has to ring off the wall before somebody finally picks it up and says, "May I help you?" in a very uninterested way, the reason all that happens is that people aren't doing their jobs.

People aren't doing their jobs. They're not keeping up their end of the deal. They're not doing what they were hired to do. That's the problem with society and business today. People aren't doing what they were paid to do.

The Number One Rule

I have a rule in business. In fact, it is my number one rule in business and life: *Do you what you said you would do, when you said you would do it, the way you said you would do it.* That's all an employer wants from its employees. That's all any employee wants from their employer. That's all any customer wants. They just want someone to do what they said they would do, when they said they would do it, the way they said they would do it.

You know what I've discovered? That's all I want from my kids. That's all I want from my spouse. That's all my spouse and kids want from me. That's all I want from my friends. Period. I want people to do what they said they would do, when they said they would do it, the way they said they would do it.

In other words, I want people to do their jobs, keep their word, live their lives, and run their business with integrity. When you do that, you show me the ultimate amount of respect. You respect me when you keep your word, and I want your respect.

Now you're probably arguing with me. You're saying, "You don't know me, Larry. You don't know how hard I work."

Yes, I do. I know exactly how hard you work. You don't work as hard you think you're working. If you own your own company, if you're a guy sitting in a home office running your own business, you think you're busting it all day long. I'll guarantee you that's not true.

You might be busy all day long, but that doesn't mean you're getting the results that you need. That doesn't mean you're accomplishing what it takes to really become successful. Just because you're busy doesn't mean you're doing the right stuff.

I'm not only talking about accomplishing the right stuff, but about understanding what your priorities ought to be in order to accomplish the right stuff. Busyness has nothing to do with accomplishment. I'm all about results. So, if you want to argue with me about how hard you're working, look at whether you're getting the right results.

Are you making the sales? Do you have the right kind of profitability in your organization? Does everyone who works with you, for you, and around you get the results that you want? Or are you a little frustrated at the end of the day?

I'll guarantee you that if you were doing the right thing, you would be getting the right results. If you're not getting the right results, it's your fault. You have to go back and look at what you're actually getting done all day long, regardless of how hard you think you're working.

Hard Work and Results

Let me give you a clue. If you're not breaking a sweat, both mentally and physically, you're not working very hard. Success at anything almost always comes down to good, old-fashioned hard work on the right things. That's the key. Are you doing the right things?

What's the right thing? This is very simple. Does it get the result you want? That's it.

Here's the problem: you don't even know what result you want. You can't sit back and say, "I want to be rich," or, "I want to weigh this amount," or "I want to have this much money," or "I'd like to make this many sales." That's not specific enough.

I want you to specifically sit down and say, "My goal for the day is to achieve THIS." Then make everything you do that day about achieving that. That's how you know whether you're doing the right thing. Establish clear priorities.

What are your priorities? If you're a salesperson, your priority is to make sales. Makes perfect sense, doesn't it? If you're a salesperson, your priority is to make sales. What goes into making sales? Obviously you have to talk to customers. You can't sell anything unless you ask somebody to buy it. So, as a salesperson, your priority must be to talk to as many customers as you possibly can so you can ask them to buy. Anything that gets in the way of doing that is not your priority because your priority is to make sales. See how simple it is?

If you're the president or owner of the company, maybe your number one priority is to meet with investors. Don't let anything get in the way of doing that.

That's the key. Know clearly what you want to accomplish for the day or week or month or year—in fact for all of those periods. Then make those things your priorities and don't let anything else get in the way.

Throw Away the To-Do List

The problem is we let things get in our way. We go to work every single day, and we sit down with our little to-do list. We think we're doing a great job because we made up this little list the day before, and we go through marking things off. That'll keep you busy, but it won't allow you to stick with your priorities and get the right thing done.

You need to throw away your to-do list. You need to get a things-that-have-to-get-done list. Get a sheet of paper and at the top put down, "Things that have to get done." Then write down the most important thing. Do that every single day. Then do whatever it takes to get those things done. Don't let anything else get in the way.

By the way, this little exercise that I've just given you is the key to all time management issues. Because this exercise isn't about managing your time but about getting the most important things done. It doesn't matter if it takes you all day. It doesn't matter if it takes you five minutes. What matters is you got the most important thing done. You established a priority clearly in advance, you went after it, and you worked on it until it was accomplished.

What if everybody who worked with you, for you, and around you did that? I'll guarantee you that you would be more successful, and you would see your results go up. If you just did it yourself, your results would improve.

I'm all about accomplishment. I don't care what you do; I want to see what you got done. Do you see the difference? This is not focusing on process. It's focusing on accomplishment. It's about results. You are paid for results. You're not paid to stay busy. You're not paid to work. You can work all day long. You're paid for the results that your efforts bring. That's it.

If you have good results, no one will care how you got them done. It doesn't have to be pretty. It just matters that you got it done. That's what I was always looking for as an employer: the guy who got things done.

Unfortunately, that's not what we judge most of the time. We sit back at the end of the day and say, "Look how busy I was. Man, I'm tired. And look how busy everybody around me was, we got a lot done!" The sad thing is sometimes you really were busy and you really are tired, and you didn't get a damn thing done.

At the end of the day, look back and ask, "Did I get the right things done?" The right things are the things that gets you the best results. Getting the best result from doing the right thing is your top priority.

When you have this as your top priority, you don't have to worry about your time or much of anything else.

The challenge you're going to face is when you know exactly what has to be done and other people get in your way. As a boss, you sit in your office, and everyone comes in and says, "Boss, I need help doing this. I need you to supervise that." You get caught up putting out other people's fires. I know that's a challenge.

This is what you have to understand: From a management standpoint, if you have people who are constantly asking you to put out their fires, teach them to put out their own fires, or teach them not to set fires. Then learn to shut the door. Become inaccessible for the small amount of time it takes to get your number one priority done. Cut yourself off from other people if it's at all possible.

Sometimes it takes eight hours to do the right thing because of interruptions. You may say, "I can't possibly cut myself off from everybody else." Oh, yes, you can. They can do without you for a little while, because that eight-hour task could probably be rolled into a half hour if it were uninterrupted time.

If people are bothering you, you could say, "Look, this is what I'm working on. I'm sure you will agree with me that this is the most important thing for me to get done today." Ask their agreement.

If you're an employee and your boss is bothering you about that most important thing and keeps stacking on more important things, just ask him: "Pick one that's the most important thing for me to get done today. You pick it, and I'll make sure it gets done." That way you've involved the other people in the process. They know what you're doing, and they know how important that one thing is. This is not a complicated process, but it can get a little nitty-gritty sometimes.

Learn how to shut the door, cut yourself off, stop communications around you, and get people on your side in accomplishing your goal. It's not that hard to do, but it will take some effort on your part.

Always know that there is plenty of time. Never complain that you don't have enough time. There's always enough time to do the right thing once the right thing has been determined and you've decided to go to work on it.

Always work faster, smarter, and harder than anyone else. Stay busy. Find things that enable you to achieve the results you really want, but remember, it's about results. It's not just about busyness. It's about accomplishment.

Stop every once in a while during your day and say, "Is this the right thing? Am I getting the best result from my actions?" These are great question to ask yourself. Then ask yourself if your contributions outweigh the cost it takes to achieve your results. It doesn't matter whether you're the CEO, whether you own your own company, or whether you're the janitor or the secretary. You have to contribute more than you cost. That's how a profit is made.

And don't ever get caught in the trap of tolerating poor performance either in yourself or others. Become very intolerant of laziness and even of busyness. Always focus on results and getting the most profitable work done.

Never lie to yourself about how busy you are or how hard you work, and never complain. The other people are trying to work. Don't involve them in your problems. Keep to yourself, to your job, to your priorities, and get the most work done.

The Hard Stuff

Success never comes down to the hard stuff. We like to think it does, but that's not true. People get the hard stuff. In fact, I never met anybody in my life that didn't get the hard stuff.

When you get hired, you're excited, you go to work, and they say, "This is your computer. This is how you enter orders," or, "This is your cash register, and this is how you operate it." Really, that's the hard stuff. That's the stuff that would challenge me the most, but everybody ends up getting that stuff because that's where we spend most of our time training. But companies don't spend a lot of time training about the simple things like taking personal responsibility, remembering that a deal is a deal, putting the customer first or making sure that we contribute more than we really cost. And they don't get the simple stuff like coming to work on time or being productive all day long doing the right things.

Often people don't respect their fellow employees. They don't respect their own time enough to take advantage of the time they're at work. They don't respect the building they work in. They use the front door as a smoke hole. They come to work looking like hoboes, because it's casual day. (Sadly, it seems now that every day is casual day.) They don't expect the best from themselves or others. They don't constantly stay focused on what has to get done.

These are very simple things that can be fixed but really have a major impact. In fact, they're so simple that most people will overlook them. You see, success doesn't come from doing the hard things. Success comes from doing the simple things really well.

Are you doing the simple things very well? Are you taking the best advantage of your time at work? Are you staying focused on the things that actually produce the results? If you are, then you're probably achieving better results than the people around you.

It's important not only to work hard but to work smart. We're there to serve others well. We're there to be nice to the people we work with. I'm not saying you have to love them all. I'm just saying be nice and respectful to the people you work with.

You need to stay optimistic. That's very different from being Mr. Happy McPositive. No one expects you to be positive about everything that happens. But me optimistic, expecting the best the outcome to happen from hard work and commitment.

Have goals. That's a very simple idea, but most people don't have goals. Stay focused. Keep learning constantly. These are simple ideas that we need to act on every single day in order to achieve what we want to achieve.

Everybody says they want it to be simple, but really we want success to be very hard, because if we buy into the idea that success is hard, then we'll have an excuse for not doing well. But I don't think there is an excuse for not doing well. I think everybody has the ability to do well, and they can when they remember that success comes from doing very simple things extraordinarily well. That's all it really takes.

In fact, if you just want to stick to one simple idea, remember Larry's number one rule for success in both business and life: Do what you said you would do, when you said you would do it, the way you said you would do it.

You Need To Get Better

When I talk about your business success, I'm really talking about you. I'm not going to let you blame business practices. I'm not going to let you talk about how your company operates or policies or procedures.

Because business success always comes down to you. Success is up to you. If you want your business to get better, know that business gets better right after the people in the business get better. In other words, your business will get better when you get better.

It works that way in every single area of any company. Sales get better right after salespeople get better. Customer service improves right after the people who deliver that customer service improve. Employees get better right after their manager gets better. And so on and so on.

In fact, everything in your life gets better when you get better, and nothing is ever going to get better until you get better. If you want your life to get better, and if you want your business to get better, then you have to get better. Wow, that sucks doesn't it! Now there is no one to blame but yourself.

There's a great line by Mark Twain: "Don't go around saying that the world owes you a living. The world owes you nothing. It was here first." Chances are the company where you work was there first too. They don't owe you a living. If you are an employee stop thinking in terms of what you are owed and start thinking in terms of what you can contribute in order to earn. That gives you the power and gets you out of your victim mentality.

I once had a receptionist who insisted on doing personal things at her desk during work hours. She would balance her checkbook, do her nails and talk to her friends on the phone. She would even have her friends come in and visit her during work hours.

When I confronted her with the problem, she told me it was her desk and she could do what she what she wanted at her desk. She actually said she was "entitled to do whatever she wanted at her desk." That was an easy fix. Thirty seconds later, it wasn't her desk anymore. Yeah, you get it. I reminded it was my desk and my company and showed her out my door.

Some employees have developed a sense of entitlement regarding their jobs, their workspace, and their company. Not surprising since we've done that in every single area of life. We grow up thinking our company owes us. We think our parents owe us. We think society owes us. We think our government owes us.

No one owes you anything. You make your own way with the best use of your time, your skills and your commitment and work. You decide the kind of life you want to live, and regardless of your circumstances, you can create the kind of life you want to live.

Sometimes, we need to remind ourselves and the people who work with us, for us and around us of that. We've become way too indulgent. We allow people to get by with way too much. And we mistakenly believe it's all about us when that's just not the case.

All of this bothers me. You know what your company owes you? A safe working environment. That's about it. As long as stuff doesn't fall on your head, then in my opinion, the company has done its part.

The company doesn't owe you an environment where you're safe from stupid people. Those people are everywhere. You can't be protected from them. Companies don't need to make sure your feelings don't get hurt. The government shouldn't have to worry about your feelings. Your family members shouldn't have to worry about your feelings. No one should have to worry about your feelings. Your feelings are up to you.

However, they should all care about your rights. I will defend your rights to the end, but I don't have the time, the money, the energy, or the desire to make sure you feel good about things. That's your choice. When you go to work every day, your company cares about your rights. That's all they have the time to care about. Your happiness is up to you.

We've become way too indulgent and coddling. We put our arms around people and say, "We're going to make sure you're happy." Good luck with that. We should never promise happiness to anybody. I can't make sure you won't get offended. I can't make sure that someone won't be or say something you disagree with. It's a cold, cruel, ugly world full of stupid people doing and saying stupid things. Suck it up, Buttercup and deal with it.

Why Your Life Sucks

Results are everything. Results are what you're ultimately going to be judged for every single time. Results are what you're paid for. Results are what you're going to be rewarded for. Your results are what society is going to look at. Know this: You created your results. Your results are your fault. The only place you get to go to lay blame is to the mirror. It was your words, your actions and your reactions that created the results you are living and that you will be judged for.

If you're one of those people who loves to whine and blame other people, stop that right now. Stop whining and complaining. Don't blame anyone else for your results. It's not their fault. Don't blame your situation in life. I don't care. I can show you people who've had it a lot worse than you do, and they're still successful. I don't want to hear how bad it is for you. No one wants to hear. They're dealing with their own stuff. Keep it to yourself. Your results are your fault.

Do yourself a favor: Stop right now and do a quick assessment. Be tough on yourself. Look at your life and your situation and then tell yourself, "This is all my fault."

When I tell people to do this, they say, "But, but, but, Larry . . ." No, there is no *but* in here. It's your fault. You created your situation. Even if some horrible thing befell you, something you had no control over, how you react to that situation it is still your fault. So, as I said with the title of my first bestselling book; *Shut up, stop whining and get a life!*

I was saying all this from the stage one day, and as I left the stage, a guy came running up to me. He said, "You know, Larry, I was watching you up there, and you look like you're doing all right, but you really don't understand. I heard everything that you said, but you really don't get it. You don't have to work with those people I have to work with. My boss is an idiot. You just don't get it, Larry. You don't have to go home to my wife, and you're not putting up with my kids." Then he put his finger up in my face—I hate it when people do that—and said, "Larry, you don't have to do what I do. You don't put up with the people I have to put up with. You just don't get it. My life sucks."

I stopped him and said, "Let me help you with this. It's because *you* suck."

Yep, sorry. If your life sucks, it's because *you* suck. I believe that little philosophy works in every single area of both life and business. If your life sucks, it's because you suck. You did it, not me. Deal with it.

This principle also works in business. If your business sucks, it's because you suck as a business-person. If your sales suck, it's because you suck as a salesperson. If your employees suck, it's because you suck as a manager. If your customer service sucks, it's because you deliver sucky customer service.

A lot of people are going to put their arm around you and say, "Honey, it's OK. It's a cold, cruel world out there and none of this has anything to do with you." No, the world is the way the world is. You can't change the world. But you can damn sure change how you look at it and respond to it and still take responsibility for everything you say and do.

If you don't like the way things are and the results you have created, then go create a new set of results. Your life doesn't have to be the way it is. Your business results don't have to be the way they are. You can choose to do things differently in order to give yourself new results.

Again, this stuff is not complicated. You have what you have because of the action you've taken. If you want new results, take new actions. That's what I'm challenging you to do.

No Excuses, No Complaints

You bought this book and you're reading it right now because you're willing to get new results. OK, then do it. Go after them. Don't offer yourself any excuses. Excuses never work. Regardless of the hand you've been dealt, learn how to play it. Play it the best you possibly can, without any whining or complaining, because people are dealing with their own stuff, and they don't want to hear you complaining. They don't want to hear you gripe. They want to see your results.

Don't talk about it; show me. And the way you show me what you've been able to accomplish is to know what you want and to go to work on it with no complaining or whining or griping. Just get out there and do it. No excuses.

Let me also shock you by telling you this right now: You like your life the way it is. No matter how bad it is, that's how you like it. That's the most alarming thing I'm probably going to tell you in this book. You like your life just the way it is. You like your results.

"No, no, Larry. I really don't. I hate it the way it is."

That's not true. If you didn't like it the way it was, you'd be actively doing something about it. Unless you're willing to tolerate the results you have, go to work and change them. It's not that hard. In fact, I'm going to give you a short list right now to get better results.

Number one, stop complaining and stop whining. The reality is that no one cares. Whining only prolongs the problem anyway.

Once you've stopped whining and have taken responsibility, you've put yourself on the road to recovery. That's really what it takes. Remember that doing better is the result of deciding to do better. You've made the decision. Prove that you really want things to be better by going to work on them.

It goes back to what I started off with: are you willing to do what it takes? If you are really committed to doing what it takes, I promise you that can achieve better results.

The rest of this book is going to be about tactics and strategies and giving you a plan that you can actually go to work on. I'm not just going to beat you up, but I have to set you up first so I can get your mind ready, so I can force you to take responsibility for where you are, take that hard look in the eye, and say, "I created this. Now what do I do?" I'm about to tell you exactly what you need to do.

You're Not Paid to Love Your Job

Business writers and speakers tell you that the key to success is just to love what you do. That's the biggest load of crap I've ever heard. I don't care whether you love your job or not; you're not paid to love your job. You're not paid to be happy on your job.

Think about this. Did you ever get a paycheck in your whole life that says down in the memo section, "We're going to pay you this time because you love it so much and because you were happy at work!"? I hope you do you're your job. And I hope you're happy on the job. But those things are bonuses and not what the paycheck is actually for.

Lots of days, I don't love what I do for a living. In fact, for a good amount of time, I hate what I do for a living. I'm primarily a professional speaker who travels the world, standing on stages and speaking to groups of people. Standing on stages takes about 100 hours a year, tops. I love my 100 hours on stage, but I have to travel 250 days a year to make those 100 hours happen. I can't tell you how much I hate those 250 days. I hate every time I have to get on an airplane, crawl in the back of a taxi, walk in the front door of a hotel, call room service, and wait for my luggage to come off the rack at the airport. I hate everything about the travel. It beats me up, but I love my 100 hours on stage. This is the key: I love the 100 hours enough to put up with the 250 days I hate.

I bet it works the same way in your job. I bet you love what you do about 10 percent of the time and hate what you do the other 90 percent of the time. Go ahead, be honest. I promise you I'm right.

You hate what you do 90 percent of the time. If that's true, then you're a regular person. That's just how it is. The key is you have to love that 10 percent. It's not fair to expect people to love what they do all day long. That's an unfair expectation, and you're going to drive yourself crazy telling yourself that one of the keys to success is to love your job. We've cheated an entire generation of people by telling them, "You'll know you're successful when you love what you do every single day." That wasn't right of us to do and we should stop it. It isn't fair to set up that level of expectation of work. Work isn't always fun. And there is going to be a huge part of it you would rather not have to go through. That's what it's called WORK. The truth is that if you truly love what you do for an hour out of the day then consider yourself luck and know that you have to love it enough to put up with the rest of it. That's the way it is in every area of life. You're not going to love what you do all the time. You're not going to be happy about what you do all the time.

Lies about Passion and Enthusiasm

Don't get sold on those great lies that people tell us about business success. Here's one: Be passionate.

Have you heard that before? I know people who are passionately wrong. I know people who are passionately stupid.

How about this one? You've heard this: enthusiasm. You just have to be enthusiastic. Just get all pumped up. Just have a great attitude. I know people who have the best attitude in the world. They're enthusiastic, they're passionate about what they do, but there's one big problem: they're no good at what they do. They're not competent. Success always comes down to competency. You have to be excellent at what you do.

You can love your job. You can be happy going to work every single day. You can be passionate and enthusiastic. You can be all of those things, and you can still be lousy at what you do. The person who's lousy at their job is not going to be successful. They're just going to be happy doing a lousy job. They're going to love the fact they're doing a lousy job.

Customers, bosses, and the world reward us for excellence in our results. It always comes down to the person who creates the best results.

I read a great book called *The War of Art*—not *The Art of War* by Sun Tzu, but *The War of Art* by Steven Pressfield. There is a great line in the book that says, "Amateurs love their jobs. Professionals love their jobs. The difference is professionals love their jobs enough to become excellent at it." That is profound! And it's exactly what people need to hear now more than ever.

Love your job. It helps, but if you're going to love your job, love it enough to become excellent at it.

Become competent first. Then work to become excellent. Then become amazing. Amazing is when you reach the very top. And your rewards increase at each level. The better you get the better your rewards will be. That's some incentive for you right there!

Congratulations. You've made it to the end of the first chapter. I'm pretty sure that I've stepped on your toes a bit.

But remember that I told you earlier that my goal was to make you uncomfortable. If I have and you've learned something then it's been well worth it.

2

How to Succeed in Business by Really Trying

People get fired, demoted, passed over for promotion and all the other bad things that happen at work for one reason more than any other reason: They didn't deserve anything better. BOOM! Yep, we get what we deserve.

If you're not getting the results that you want in life and in business, it just might be because you're not working hard enough. You haven't become invaluable to your customers. You haven't become invaluable to your company. You're not worth enough for things to be better.

So how do you increase your worth? How do you become invaluable? Let me tell you a quick story.

I ship everything from my favorite UPS store. I have a lot of stuff coming in and out. I order a lot of crazy things. I'm a great shopper, and I like to have water buffalo skulls to hang on the walls of my house. You name it, I get it.

I've gotten to know the people at my UPS store very well. There was one person at the store that was just the best! Her name was Carolyn. She became my shipping queen. She handled everything for me. When you have a lot of stuff going in and out, you have to be able to trust the person you're working with.

It got to the point that I relied on her completely. I could walk in and say, "Carolyn, make sure this happens," and I was confident it would happen. She's listened to my stuff. She read my books. She watched me when I was on television. She "got me." As a result, we became friends, and when I wanted something done, I knew that I all I had to do was walk in the front door, ask for Carolyn, and it would get handled.

One day as I was approaching the front door, I saw a "Help Wanted" sign. I walked in and asked, "Is someone leaving, or are you just hiring more people?"

Carolyn said, "Larry, I'm the one that's leaving." I fell on the floor and cried. (Well, not really, but I was really disappointed.)

"Carolyn, what am I going to do?" We were buddies. She watched out for me. She took care of me. Although I was happy for her because she was going on to bigger and better things, I was sad for myself. I was worried about my stuff. I was very selfish, and that's the way customers are. They're selfish. They're worried about their stuff.

"Don't worry, Larry," she said. "You'll be fine. These other people are great. They'll take good care of you." But my confidence in the whole organization was shaken simply because Carolyn was leaving. As a matter of fact, I told my wife that we might have to go to a different UPS store, one closer to our house, because now it didn't matter where we went. She said, "Larry, let's just hang in and not do anything yet. Let's give the other folks a chance." She is the calm one as you can see!

Time passed. Sure enough, the new people were all able to handle my business just fine. Fine, but not like Carolyn. They were good, they were competent, and they gave me great service, but they were not like Carolyn. We didn't have that connection. I counted on her. I relied on her.

I didn't even think of it as the UPS store. UPS had nothing to do with it. It was the place I took my stuff so Carolyn could take care of it for me.

Carolyn put herself in front of the organization she worked for. She was my contact. She was the one who shipped things for me. It didn't matter whether Carolyn worked for UPS, ABC, or QRT. It did not matter. The most important thing to me was that I had somebody I could trust. She became *invaluable*.

What made her so invaluable to me? She worked hard to get to know who I was. She always gave me a smile. Every once in a while she would hand me a Hershey's kiss when I walked in the front door, and believe me, that's about all it takes to keep me happy. She went out of her way to establish a connection with me, and over a period of time, she proved that I could trust her. Her competence came to the forefront. I knew that I could always get what I wanted if I just went to Carolyn. She was competent, then became excellent, then amazing! She became more important to me than the company she worked for.

What are you doing to make sure that you become invaluable to your company and to your customers? What are you doing to go the extra step to make sure you know who your customer is and to let your customer know that you're the person they can rely on?

If you're just a face in the crowd, believe me, it's easy to pass you over and consider you as "just another employee." But if you're the one person people ask for, that they want to talk to, that they need to make sure that they get the results they're looking for, then you're going to become invaluable to your company. And the good news is that it's just not that hard. Remember that I've already told you that it's not the big things or the hard things; it's the simple things.

I work a couple of times a year in Boston. When I go to Boston, I like to eat seafood. I'm from Arizona, where we don't get a lot of fresh seafood. There's one little restaurant that I always go to. When I walked in the door of this restaurant for the very first time, I just sat at the bar, because when I'm by myself, I don't normally get a table.

The bartender came up and said, "What's your name and what do you do for a living?" I told him. We talked for a few seconds. He got me my drink. He got me my food. I always order the same thing when I'm there. I like their clam chowder and I like their crab cakes. And he brought me my order of chowder and crab cakes within a few minutes.

His name was Hugh. Hugh the bartender. Six months later, I walked in the front door. Hugh looked up, saw me, and said, "Larry, good to have you back. Can I get you your regular?" I was amazed that he knew my name. I was more amazed that he knew what I liked to eat. Sure enough, he set down my drink and then he set down my crab cakes and chowder about as soon as I confirmed I would have my regular.

I asked him, "Hugh, how in the world did you remember who I was and what I eat and drink?"

"Larry, when I decided to come to work here, I decided there's one thing I could do better than anyone else. While I can't out-hustle all these guys back here serving food and drinks, I'll guarantee you I can remember people's names better. So, that was my goal. Just remember people's names when they come in and try to remember something about them."

I've been going there for four or five years now. Every time I walk in the front door, Hugh remembers who I am, what I eat, and what I drink. I'm amazed by that, even though it's a very simple thing. I asked, "Hugh, how's that work for you?"

"You know," he said, "sometimes I think they keep me around just because I know everybody who comes in." He also told me that he gets a lot better tips as a result. I can assure you that's true. You tip somebody a little more money when they know you by name, when they know who you are, and they know something about you. It pays off. It always pays off to go that extra mile.

Here's the good news. It's not very crowded in that extra mile and it doesn't take much to impress people these days. That may be sad, but it's a very easy thing for you to capitalize on. All you have to do to become invaluable to a customer is pay attention to who they are. Listen to them. That's a simple thing you can do. Use their name. Is that tough? No, it's not.

What are you doing right now to become invaluable to the people you work with, for, and around? You have to become invaluable to your company. You need to become invaluable to your coworkers. You especially have to become invaluable to your customers. This works for you, no matter who you are. It doesn't matter who you are or what you do for a living.

Everybody has customers, and you have to serve them well. The best way to serve them is to figure out what you can do to become invaluable to them. It's not hard, but it's going to take a little extra effort.

That's the problem. People aren't willing to put in extra effort. They're not willing to work very hard on their jobs, and they're certainly not willing to work very hard on themselves.

This is my approach: You have to work harder on yourself than you do on your job. That may sound strange to you, because so far I've been beating you up about working hard on your job. Yes, that's important, but remember what I said? Business gets better when the people in the business get better.

In other words, you have to get better. You have to work harder on who you are in addition to getting better at how well you do your job. It's not up to your employer to make sure that you're becoming a better person, that parts up to you.

What does it take to become a better person? Get out a sheet of paper right now and write down the last five books you've read. If you're challenged by that, that's a clue for you. You're not working very hard on yourself.

As I've said, in the last twenty-five years, I've read nearly four thousand books. I'm not asking you to do that, but anybody can read a book a month. Who can't read a book a month? Here's what you're going to say: "Oh, but, Larry, you don't understand. There's just no time."

Of course, there's time. Years ago, I heard someone say that the average billionaire has the same amount of time as the average bum. It's just how they choose to spend their time. You're not choosing to spend your time in ways that will make you a better person.

First of all, you can start reading more. There's amazing information out there that you can get just from picking up a book and skimming through it.

What do you do when you read a book? This is sort of an aside, but I'm going to give you a lesson about reading a book. Read for intent, not for content. I don't care so much what the book has to say; I want to know what the book's trying to teach me. What was the one thing the author wanted me to know? What was the author's intention? That's worth some gold right there. You don't need a hundred good ideas from any book. You need one.

One great idea is all you need to take you to a much better place. One idea is all it takes to make you wildly successful.

Find one idea from every conversation you have, every book you read, every seminar you go to, every speech you listen to. And when you get your one idea. Write it down. Then later, review it and think about how you can apply that idea to your life and business.

In fact, that's a great goal for this book. What's the one idea you've gotten so far? Write it down. And when you get to the end of this book, write down the one, over-whelming, actionable idea that you can apply to your life. Then go to work on it.

Stop saying there is no time and go read some books by people who can teach you something. There's plenty of time if it's important enough. And trust me, it's important enough. There's plenty of time to do the most important thing, whether it's improving your business or improving you. The most important thing for you to do for yourself is to better at who you are and what you do. The better you are as a person, the better you will be as an employee, as an employer, an entrepreneur, a husband, a wife, a father, mother or friend. Remember that everything gets better when you get better and nothing is really doing to get better until you get better!

So, what are you doing right now to get better? Take a minute, take a sheet of paper, and write down what you're doing to get better. Write down the books you're reading, the audio programs you're listening to, the kind of television you watch and the YouTube and other videos you watch. Great information is everywhere. There are more opportunities to learn now than ever before. Don't waste them.

Now: once you have your list, you're probably going to say, "You know, Larry, my list is not very full. I need to be doing more." You're right. Go do more.

TNT: Today, Not Tomorrow

When would be a good time to start on a good idea? That's simple, isn't it? Right now. Today. That's the time to start on your good idea. You're probably thinking, "But, but Larry, I have a lot of things planned today. You don't understand. You see, I have to stop by the cleaners, and then I have to go by the grocery story on the way home to get some bread and some milk, and then when I get home, oh, man, Larry, I'm really going to be tired. I have to kick back for a little while, watch a little television, and then I have to fix dinner then I have to sit down with the family and spend a little family time. Then I have to get some sleep! After all, I work hard, and I'm beat!"

I don't care. Your big list of excuses doesn't really matter. Here's what you have to do: today you have to get started on becoming a better version of who you are. Today. Not tomorrow. Again: Today. Not. Tomorrow. TNT. That's the key idea. Start now.

There's a great quote from General George S. Patton, who said, "A good idea implemented today is better than a perfect idea implemented tomorrow." I've built my business on it. I've changed my life based on that one quote. I am known for having an idea and just starting it right then. No waiting. No hesitation. Right now.

So, do it today. Always today. You may say, "I don't have the time." Or you may be one of those people who says, "I have plenty of time." No, you don't. There's no time. There's absolutely no time. There is no time better than now.

If you want to increase your sales, when would be a great time to start calling more customers? How about next month? No, that won't work. Wait until next month and the opportunity might have passed you by. You need to start calling today.

If you have an employee that's done a great job, when would be a great time to go over and say thank you? Not tomorrow. You'd want to do that today, wouldn't you? If you have an employee that's absolutely incompetent, and they're ruining your business, insulting your customers, and causing chaos, when do you want to get rid of that employee? Not tomorrow. You want to do it today.

When should you start doing anything that's really worth doing? You need to do it today, not tomorrow. Never tomorrow. Always today. Remember this. TNT: *today, not tomorrow*. There's no time. Do it today.

You might be saying, "It's going to take more time for me to get ready." No, it isn't. You need to work fast. Speed will keep you on track. You need to work as fast as you possibly can.

Let me tell you why speed is important. When you work out of a sense of urgency, you will work from your gut. Your gut will do the right thing before you can outthink yourself.

I'm not saying go off half-cocked, but the more you plan and strategize, the more likely you are to start taking shortcuts. You're going to say, "We could save a little over here. We could do this over there." Don't do that. Instead just get started. By the time you have strategized about your task, chances are you could have probably already finished.

Work fast, do it now, create a sense of urgency. Remember, there's no time. You have to get it done. When you expect to get the work done quickly, it will get done quickly. That's what I've discovered, and it's amazing. Work takes as much time as you'll allow for it. If you don't allow much time to get the work done, it won't take much time to get it done.

Get started right now improving your life.

Be Very Selfish

Let's say you've done everything that I've talked about so far. For example, you've decided to become invaluable to people. There's a huge upside to that for sure. But there is also a downside. I know, how could there be a downside? Because people are people. Because if you're the person who's going the extra mile, if you're really working harder than everybody else, if you're the one that your customers always call and ask for, I can promise you that your coworkers will make fun of you. They're going to talk behind your back. They're going to criticize you. They're going to call you a kiss-up. Who cares? You're not working to support their family; you're working to support *your* family.

Be very selfish when it comes to work. You're there to promote *you*. You're living *your* life. It's *your* success we're talking about. You don't need to be one of the pack. You need to be out in front of the pack through your outstanding efforts.

The person who does a mediocre job gets mediocre results. You're tired of mediocrity; that's why you're reading this book.

Step out in front. You do that by working harder and smarter than anyone else, by spending some time and money on yourself. You do it by reading books, listening to programs, going to lectures, spending the few extra minutes that it takes to set yourself apart from everyone else.

Most people aren't willing to do that. That's why you're doing it: you don't want the results that most people get. You're sick of that kind of results. You want more, but you're going to take criticism about it. Big deal. Move past the criticism and remind yourself every single day that you're doing this for *you*, because you want more out of life. To heck with what they want. That's their life and that's their problem and those are their lousy results.

To summarize, here's what it takes to really become invaluable: Spend more time on making yourself better. Figure out what it takes to be successful in every area of life. Understand what it takes to set priorities. Spend some time establishing goals and figuring out what it takes to achieve those goals. Read some books, some great biographies of people who have been successful, and figure out what you can learn from them.

Remember, it only takes one good idea to change where you are—one good idea to make you wealthy, to make you better at who you are and what you do.

Know everything you can about your company, its product line, and how its business is conducted so you can become a valuable resource to your customer by knowing what your company really does, what it provides and the problem it solves. Know what your competition has to offer so you can provide a reliable comparison when asked.

Understand your customers. Understand that your customers want to be listened to. They want to be recognized. They want to be identified with. Start thinking from the customer's perspective. Understand their problem and their pain and what you and your company and products can do to solve that problem and alleviate that pain.

And don't just work hard, learn to work fast. Have a sense of urgency. Remember, there's not enough time to get it all done. You have to establish priorities and do the most important things, and you have to do those things very quickly, so learn to work fast.

Then pursue excellence in all things. It's about excellence. The one who wins in the long run is the one who's the best at what they do and serves others by doing it.

Your Sacred Workplace

I want to talk about the physical place you work—the office building or retail establishment you go to work in. I don't care if it's the place down the hall in your house that used to be your third bedroom.

If that's where you go to work, that's the place I'm talking about right now.

Here's the credo for that place, and you need to learn this credo and be able to say it: This is a sacred place, where we only speak well of ourselves, we only speak well of our organization, we only speak well of our competitors, and we only speak well of our customers.

Start to think of those walls where you go to work as a sacred place. You may laugh and say, "No, Larry, this is not a sacred place. This is a place where they expect too much of me. This is a place where people gripe at me because there's not enough getting done. This is a place where I don't have the resources I used to have because we've been cutting back and downsizing and resizing.

"You don't know those idiots I have to work with. My boss is a pain in the butt all day long. That's the place I work. You don't understand that third bedroom. I have kids banging on the door back there all day, Larry. It's a little hard to think of it as a sacred place."

Doesn't matter. You need to understand that the place where you work is a sacred place because that's where you work hard and earn the money to finance the rest of your life.

Let me talk to you a moment about sacred places. Let's say you walked in the door of St. Patrick's Cathedral in New York City. I don't care who you are, and I don't care what your religious background is. You could be the biggest atheist on two feet. But if you walk in that place, I promise you will not think of cussing, telling a dirty joke, or spitting on the floor. You wouldn't do anything in a profane because you would know that it is a sacred place whether you agree with the belief system it represents or not.

That's what you have to do with your workplace as well. You have to treat it like a sacred place.

Furthermore, when that idiot coworker of yours says something stupid to the customer and now you have to solve that customer's problem, you're not going to call that coworker an idiot anymore. I know you want to, and you may do it in private later, but to the customer, you're going to say something totally different. You're going to treat that coworker with respect, because we only speak well of each other in our sacred place.

You don't get to make fun of another department or another coworker, because that's not what your customer needs to hear. They need to only hear you speak well of each other.

I wanted to buy a new television. I walked in this big retail store where I picked out the one I wanted. It was a lot of money, but I was totally in. A clerk approached me, and I told him that I wanted to buy that TV.

The clerk said, "I don't think we have any of those, but I'll go check." He went and checked, came back, and said, "No, the computer says we don't have any."

"Well," I said, "you're part of a great big chain. I bet you could call around and check to see if some of the other stores have it."

"I'll go check the inventory."

He came back in a few minutes and said, "Yes, the computer tells me that a store about fifteen minutes from here has it, but usually that inventory is wrong. You can't always trust the inventory count on the computer."

I am standing there expecting more information to come out of him, but that was all the clerk had to say. I said, "Could you go check with them? Could you call them to make sure they really have it? Couldn't they walk in the back to see if it's there before we drive across town to go get this television?"

He huffed and puffed and let out a big old sigh, and he walked away. In a few minutes, he came out with a sheet of paper with a phone number written on it and handed it to us.

"What's that?" I said.

"That's the phone number," he said. "If you want to find out, you can call them."

"You know, that seems more like your job than mine. Why don't you call them?"

"It takes them forever to answer. Then, when you finally get them on the phone, they don't know what they're talking about."

What kind of confidence did that build in me? I'm going to call a place to find out if I can spend $4,000 with them, and I know it's going to take them forever to answer, and they're not going to know what they're talking about when they do answer. That made me feel great about this whole thing.

I told the clerk to go and make the call, because it didn't look to me as if he was all that busy, and before I drove across town and spent that kind of money, I wanted to make sure that the TV was really there. Again, he sighed, and he huffed and puffed, and he wandered off. Finally, he came back and said, "You're right. They don't have it either. It took them forever, and they don't have it either."

OK, they didn't have the TV either, so I didn't have to drive across town so there's that. But did I need to hear the clerk bad-mouth a store owned by his company? Did that build confidence in me as a customer? Did that make me want to ever walk in the door of their entire chain again?

No, it didn't. I didn't need to know what that guy thought of that other store. I didn't need to know how long it took them to answer and I certainly didn't need to learn that they probably didn't know what they were talking about anyway. That was information that I, as the customer, didn't need to hear. It didn't build up my confidence in the organization. In fact, it made it impossible for me to spend money there. I went to another company because TVs aren't that hard to get, and they happily took my money with no issues.

I don't care what you have to offer, I can get it someplace else and I can probably get it cheaper, faster and from somebody who's a whole lot friendlier and nicer and may know more than you. That's just the reality of the world we live in. In fact, I can go online and get it and never even have to talk to a human and have it delivered by tomorrow. So, you have to go out of your way to please me when you have me in front of you, on the phone or even on your website. So, go out of your way to respect yourself, your company and your coworkers.

You also have to speak well of your competitors. Now you're saying, "That doesn't even make any sense. How am I supposed to sell people what I have to offer if I'm not going to tear down the competition?"

First of all, you don't ever build yourself up by tearing someone else down. Don't spend any time tearing down the competition. You need to know what your competition has to offer. You need to know what they sell, how they sell it, what their product does in comparison to yours, what their service is. It's going to take some work, it's going to take some effort, but you have to know your competition. Regardless, you don't bad-mouth your competition.

In fact, I love it when a company openly praises their competition. I actually think more of both companies when that happens. Nothing builds confidence in a company and its abilities more than when they say something like, "You know, that's not really what we're best at. We could do it, but you probably ought to call XYZ Company if you really want a great job."

I appreciate that. I want to do business with the best company, and when a company tells me they're not the best ones to do that, I'm happy to go to someplace else, and then I'll do my best to make sure

I spend money with the company who told me that. It's not a hard thing to do. Just don't tear other people down. Remember, you build yourself up all on your own, and you don't build yourself up by tearing other people down.

Respect: The Ultimate Key

You also have to speak well of the customer. I was checking into a hotel in Orlando, Florida. I'm standing there at the front desk. Two front-desk clerks: one is helping me, the other one is on the phone. I hear every word that the one on the phone has to say. She's trying to tell a customer how to get to her hotel. She is frustrated, and finally she screams at him, "I don't know north from south. I know right from left. That's all I know. Tell me what's around you."

Obviously the customer tells her what he's sitting in front of. She says, "I don't know where that is. Tell me something else." She's screaming and yelling at this guy. She says, "Hold on a minute." She puts him on hold, turns to the other clerk, and says, "He's an idiot. He can just sit there on the phone for all I care."

"Why is he an idiot?" I asked. "At least he knows north from south. That's something you don't know."

By the way, I'm one of those guys who has an over-whelming impulse to point out things like that. Because it bothers me. I believe that if you see or experience bad service that you have to speak up, and this was truly bad service.

"You know," I said, "he's ultimately going to find his way to this hotel, whether you help him or not, because he has a reservation. When he checks in, he's going to be spending money at this hotel, and when he does, it winds its way around until it eventually gets back to paying your salary. This guy that you've just yelled at and called an idiot, he's going to pay your salary this week. You shouldn't speak ill of a customer and certainly not in front of another customer. By the way, what are you going to say about me when I walk off?"

She looks at me, says, "Oh, brother!" and wanders off into the back.

I'm left standing there talking to the other clerk. I say, "Could I have her name? I'm going to call her supervisor. I want to report that whole thing."

She says, "I'm her supervisor."

I couldn't believe it! I said, "*You're* her supervisor?"

She said, "That's right. I'm her supervisor. You don't understand how hard it is to get good people."

"Well," I say, "I bet that's what your manager says about you too."

She didn't have a sense of humor about that. (I find that a lot when I'm doing this kind of thing. People don't have the same sense of humor I have.) She was willing to condone bad behavior. She was willing to let one of her employees treat a customer badly in front of another customer. That's absolutely unacceptable. And she didn't know one of my maxims: What you condone you endorse.

Never speak ill of a customer. Customers pay your salary. Customers keep you in business. Customers make you profitable. Remember, you are nothing but an expense. Don't ever think of yourself as anything but an expense. I don't care whether you're a one-person shop or whether you work for a company that has thousands of employees. Either way, you still have customers and those customers keep you in business. A customer represents revenue. Therefore, the last person that you ever ought to speak ill of is the person in charge of your revenue.

All of this really comes down to respect. You have to respect the people you work with. You have to respect your customer. You have to respect the space you work in enough to deliver the right kind of service that keeps you profitable. Is that hard to understand? If it is, perhaps you need to rethink things.

Are you respecting the place you work? If I pulled up in front of your business, I could tell in a second whether you respect your workplace or not. If you have a bunch of employees standing out in front of your front door smoking cigarettes then you don't respect the place where you're working.

If I walk in the front door and the carpet is stained, you don't respect your workplace. If I go in the restroom at your business, and it's dirty, there's no respect here. Are there cigarette butts by the front door? Then you don't care enough about my business even to sweep out your entryway. I'll go someplace else.

"Larry, that's not fair." You know what? I don't have to be fair. I'm the customer. It's my money. I get to choose where I spend it, and I will choose to spend it where people respect their space enough to keep it clean.

That's all it comes down to. I have the money. I'm in charge. Prove to me that you are worth my money by at least keeping your place clean. Is that too much to ask?

At this point, maybe you're saying, "Larry, you are getting awfully picky." Again, it's my money. I have the right to be picky and I don't have to be fair about how I spend my money.

If I go in a restaurant and all I can smell is cleaning solution, that tells me that they at least mopped the floor, but I didn't go to a restaurant to have a dinner that smells like cleaning solution. They should have figured out some way to keep it clean without having me smell that disinfectant.

If I go to a restaurant, and there's paper on the floor or worse, then don't be surprised if I never go back there again. Crumbs on the floor tells me you're not interested in keeping your place clean. If you can't keep it clean out front, then I don't even want to know what your kitchen looks like.

Yes, I'm being picky. Customers need to be pickier. I'll talk a lot more about that when I talk about customer service in a later chapter, but I'm telling you right now, respect the place you work enough to keep it clean.

If I come into your office and I walk up to your desk and it's a mess, that's a problem. And don't tell me that all those piles of paper help you get more work done. That's a lie. You're kidding yourself. Clean that thing off. You can't stay focused on one thing when you're surrounded by a hundred more things. Don't tell me that's just how you do things.

I'm trying to teach you a better way to do things and I promise you will get more done in a clean office with a clean desk. If you put one project in front of you, you will stay more focused and the project will get done faster. You achieve more and you accomplish more by staying focused. You can't focus on a hundred things at once. Clean off your desk and focus on one thing. It's a simple, little fix that reaps huge results.

In fact, here's how I'm going to summarize my whole view of respect: you build respect in your organization from the ground up, and I mean literally from the ground up.

Look at the floor. If the floor is dirty, if your parking lot is dirty, if your office is a mess, if your trash cans are overflowing, if the top of your desk is covered with papers and mess and stuff from the lunch that you had three hours ago, then you don't respect your place. Build respect in your organization from the ground up.

Respect your coworkers, especially in front of your customers. Respect other customers, especially in front of your customers. Respect your competitors especially in front of your customers.

Show respect verbally and physically. Show respect in your attitude toward your customer and the people you work with. If you show me respect as your customer, I'll show you respect and probably spend more money with you.

A Roster of Idiots

Idiots are inside every organization. You can't be protected from them. They're on the streets, they're at church, they're in the grocery store, they're everywhere, and it's unrealistic to think they're not going to be sitting in the cubicle right next to you. Trust me, they're there. I even wrote a New York Times bestseller entitled, *People Are Idiots And I Can Prove It*. Great book. Easiest book I ever wrote. Because idiots are everywhere and so is the evidence of their existence.

You have to learn how to deal with these folks. There are stupid people everywhere who are going to hurt your feelings, tick you off and make you mad.

I work with lots of different companies. A lot of times when I go in to speak, the president of the company will come up to me and say, "Yeah, Larry, we're just one, big, happy family around here."

Yeah, right. Is this guy blind or just ignorant? Look around. You can tell in a minute that you're not one, big, happy family. Your business is like all families and all families have their share of idiots. Look at your own family, right? There's always that one relative that everyone else knows is an idiot.

So, your business is no different. You will have coworkers who are idiots who say and do stupid things. Part of your job is to figure out how to get along with them. And you are going to have to be very adept as there are all kinds of problem children in your little business family.

Let me give you some of the categories. Number one, there's the liar. You know whom I'm talking about; the person who lies even when it's easier to tell the truth. When I was growing up, my dad told me that he would rather have a thief working for him than a liar, because at least you can watch a thief.

The worst thing you can do to me is lie. If I find somebody who works for me is lying to me, I fire them immediately. If someone I do business with lies to me, I fire them too. That's how it is. No exceptions and no questions asked. You don't get to lie to me. That character flaw bleeds through into other areas of life and business, so I don't tolerate a liar.

You're going to work with people who lie to you. You're going to have to decide how you are going to handle it based on your core values. But here is the most important thing—never be the liar someone else has to deal with.

Then there's this one and I love this one: the person who cries all the time. They come in and say, "Boo-hoo," and they have to tell you how sad it all is. I remember what Tom Hanks said in the movie *A League of Their Own*: "There's no crying in baseball."

There's no crying in business either. Crying is a form of manipulation. I have no tolerance for someone who can't sit in front of me and tell me what the problem is without crying about it. If you come in and tell me that you just got a phone call and your dog was run over then we'll both sit down and cry together. But if you're going to come in and cry to me because some coworker down the hall hurt your feelings then just keep it to yourself. Handle it yourself. I don't want to know about it. Put on your big boy pants and handle your feelings.

On the opposite side of that spectrum, you have Mr. Happy, Mr. Positive Attitude, Mr. Every Cloud Has a Silver Lining, Mr. I Have a Cliché for Everything. I've renamed this guy Mr. You Make Me Sick. I can't stand this kind of person.

Give me Mr. Negative, who gets the job done. That's what I'm looking for: the person who gets the best results. I want Mr. Crappy Attitude, who's sick and tired of incompetence and slacking off and wants to get some work done. That's the guy I want working for me.

I'll take Mr. Crappy Attitude over Mr. Positive Attitude any time. Don't give me a cliché. Don't come up to me when we're facing a real crisis in business and say, "But, Larry, you don't understand. Every cloud has a silver lining." Sometimes that silver lining is a tornado, and it tears the hell out of things. And never say to me, "Larry, we don't have problems here. We have opportunities." You've heard that. That whole idea makes me sick. Sometimes problems are just that. They're problems! And you have to see them as problems in order to fix them. You have to tackle them, face them, and grab hold of them like they are serious and not a cliché.

Then you have the person who is so sweet that they want to make you puke—Little Suzy Sweetheart or Bubbly Bob, who says, "Is Mr. Grumpy having a bad day?" Get the hell out of my face! I have work to do.

I can't stand this kind of person, because I've discovered this person is sweet to your face and will be the first to stab you in the back. You've probably been stabbed in the back by Good Ol' Bubbly Bob before. I know I have.

Then you have the gossip—the person who runs up and down the hall and can't wait to tell you everything that's going on in somebody else's life. This person doesn't get much work done. How could they? They're information central. They're the person who has all the word on everybody. They are the *National Enquirer* of your business. They know everybody's business, and they can't wait to pass on any bad news about your coworkers to you and everybody else.

To deal with a gossip, cut them off. Instantly. The minute they start in, say, "You know, this is a sacred place, where we only speak well of each other. We only speak well of the customer and a place where we're going to honor by respecting everyone in it." That'll cut them off. Then they'll bad-mouth you, but who cares?

Then you have the bully. Bullies come in all shapes and sizes. In business, it's not like the bully on the playground. Bullies on the playground were easy to spot as they were probably bigger than you. But sometimes the bully in a business can be that sweet, little, gray-haired receptionist who won't transfer your calls.

Bullies have fragile little egos. They can't gain power through their talents, so they use whatever else they have at their disposal. Sometimes they rub your nose in their title. "I'm the vice president," or "I'm the boss, and you're going to do what I say because I'm the boss."

When I was growing up, the last thing I wanted to ever hear from my mom was, "Because I said so" when I asked why I couldn't do something. There are still guys running businesses today who get things done because they said so.

Don't be a bully, and if you're dealing with a bully, understand that bullies thrive on fear and run from confidence. Speak with confidence, look them in the eye, and you can usually back them down in a hurry.

Now let me give you another category of idiots. This is a very special category that I know you've dealt with.

A Category of Asses

This whole category has a lot of subcategories, and this group of people are the asses. You know whom I'm talking about.

First of all, there's the *smart-ass*. He has a smart-ass remark for everything. When the remark is made in good humor, it can relieve a lot of tension and it's a good thing, but when it's done in a mean, sarcastic way, smart-asses become irritants that keep you from your goal. Be careful of them.

Then you have the *hard-ass*. This is the person who never had a good day in their whole life. They gripe about everything. Nothing is ever good enough to suit them. They take the hardest line possible about everything. They don't know how to make the punishment fit the crime.

Sometimes you just need to stop the hard-ass and tell them to lighten up. Remind them of perspective. Maybe they'll come around. Maybe they won't.

Then you have—this person is kind of like Suzy and Bob. This is the *kiss-ass*. This person is easy to recognize. That's the person who has brown on their nose. The brown-noser is everyone's very best buddy. They want to be liked and will do whatever it takes to make that happen.

They're ones in charge of the birthday parties. They're the ones who put a little valentine on everyone's desk on Valentine's Day. Again, this person will probably stab you in the back. They'll suck up to your face but be careful once you walk on by.

Then you have the next category of asses. This is the *dumbass*. They say and do things that are inappropriate. They say dumb things, they do dumb things, and God love them, there's just not much you can do about them. Shake your head in bewilderment and stay out of their way.

Then you have the *jackass*. There are lots of these folks around. You could name a dozen right now. If this person works for you, I suggest you fire them. Life's too short to work with a jackass. If you're working for a jackass, go find another job. Life is just too short to spend it working for a jackass. Move on. But you may have some coworkers who fall in this category and you have no choice but to learn to work around this person.

The last category of ass is the *cute-ass*. This is the person who's trying to get by just by being cute. These are the folks who have little talent but have gotten by on their cute looks or cute little attitude since they were babies.

Am I jealous? Maybe. Just a little bit. Because they're getting by on their cuteness. They have no real skill. This is a special kind of idiots that can combine all of the other kinds and get by with it simply because of their cuteness. This is a person you have to be careful of. While people should always judge others based on their contribution, this person makes no contribution and yet it still works out for them. Beware.

You know the people I've been talking about here? Sure you do. I bet you can think of examples of each one of these categories and you can come up with a name that will slide right into that category. You're asking, "What should I do about all these idiots I have to work with?"

Remember this: all idiots are self-absorbed. They're all caught up in who they are. They don't care much about you, and they don't care much about their company. They're into themselves, and they're interested only in themselves. They have fragile little egos that need to be fed.

If you have to work with them starve them. Starve their egos. It's like an Internet troll. Starve them and they die off. Don't give the idiots the satisfaction of giving them your peace of mind. As Marianne Williamson says, "When you give someone a piece of your mind, you give up your peace of mind."

That doesn't mean you don't stand up to them and make your case with confidence. But you don't have to be a jerk about it either. Just confront them with the way they're treating you and the way they're treating others and say, "Your method might work with them, but it doesn't work with me. We both have a goal here and the goal is to get the job done. I would appreciate you working with me to get the job done, and if you're not able to do that, please stay out of my way."

In other words, be very honest, up-front, polite, but firm. That's the rule for dealing with idiots. Don't reduce yourself to their level. Rise above them. When they get mad, ignore them or laugh, but don't fight with them.

As the saying goes, "When you fight with a pig, you both get dirty, but the pig likes it." When you fight with an idiot, you're both going to get dirty, but they will win, because you've reduced yourself to their level, and they enjoy it.

Here's the ugly truth: Sometimes, like it or not, you're an idiot too. Yeah, I know that's hard to admit, but you are. You have every one of the traits that I've just talked about. You slide through these categories yourself. You're having a bad day, and you're a jackass. You have days where you just say things that you wish you hadn't said and you're a dumbass. Sometimes you're going to be a bully and sometimes you're going to be prone to gossip a little bit.

You are just as guilty as they are. The key is to recognize it quickly in yourself and move back to the kind of person you really want to be. That's how you deal with idiots, and that's how you deal with yourself.

Understand this: Everybody makes mistakes. Everybody messes up. You're going to mess up. You're going to find yourself in a situation where you've messed up, and you have to go to someone, maybe your boss, or your coworker or maybe your customer, and say, "I'm an idiot. I messed up, and I'm sorry."

The first thing to understand is that you have to admit where you are. You have to take responsibility for your situation and your role in it. You have to clarify quickly what you did that made it happen, but always remember this: If you're going to someone to admit that you've made a mistake or that a mistake has been made, go in with a plan. Take responsibility for the problem, or at least your role in it, but always go in with a plan. Everybody's going to forgive you much more quickly if you say, "This is what happened. This is my role in it. I'm sorry that we are where we are, but this is the plan I have to fix it."

If you have a plan to fix it, you can defuse the situation, get past the problem and your role in it, and move on to a solution. Bosses want solutions. Customers want solutions. Everyone should want a solution. When you present the problem, always present the solution at the same time. Otherwise, you haven't done anything but a rehash of the problem.

Ethics in Black-and-White

Let's talk about ethics. Ethics is black-and-white. That's a problem, because we live in a society that's bathed in gray. I don't believe in gray. I believe that life really is black-and-white. I think it's either right or it's wrong, it's either good or it's bad, you're either in the way or on the way, it's either hello or good-bye.

But that's not how most people live, that's not how we run our businesses, and that's not what we've learned to expect in our society. We all walk that fine line, with one foot in the white and one foot in the black, so we live in a gray area. That is not acceptable when you're running a business. That's how we end up with all the problems that we see on the six o'clock news, such as CEOs that are going to prison because of unethical business practices.

Those practices drive themselves down to a very mundane level in our businesses. It's amazing at what we've come to accept in our society today. One survey said that 14 percent of employees think it's OK to take office supplies home for personal use; in other words, they think it's okay to steal It's not okay. It's stealing. It doesn't belong to you. These people should be fired as they are thieves. Too tough? Too bad. What if this person came to your house for dinner and thought it was okay to steal silverware? Would you tolerate it? No. You wouldn't.

Lots of other things are unethical. For instance, lying on your résumé. Or saying you have a doctor's appointment when you really went to get a haircut.

Making personal phone calls at work. Are you paid to make personal phone calls at work? If you're not paid to do it, you shouldn't be doing it.

Using the company copier for your personal stuff. It's not your paper, and you are doing it on company time, so you don't get to do that.

Participating in office gossip. I've already talked about being a gossip. That's unethical. Calling in sick when you aren't. That's unethical too. And it's stealing. Coming in five minutes late or showing up late for an appointment. Unethical. Taking a seventy-five-minute lunch hour when you are only allowed an hour. An hour is sixty minutes, not seventy-five minutes. You stole again.

I draw a hard line on all of these things because I've run a company. I know you have to stay profitable and you don't stay profitable when you let these little things slide. You can't let any unethical behavior slide.

The Decline and Fall of a Restaurant

Let me give you an example. I know this has happened to you. You see a new restaurant open and you are excited to go. It's pretty good. In fact, you like it a lot. You tell them you're going to come back, because the service was so good, and the food was delicious.

Two months later, you go back. It's not quite as good as it was the time before. You go back sixty days after that and it's barely mediocre. The waiter doesn't take good care of you. Nobody comes by to check on you. You notice a little smudge on the fork or crumbs on the table from the previous diner. It takes a little too long to get waited on. The food isn't quite as good either.

Three months from now, you're driving past, and you see that they're closed. There's a "For Lease" sign in front of the building. What happened? Let me tell you what I think happened.

One day an employee didn't pay much attention to one customer, and while his boss noticed, she didn't say anything about it. She let it slide. Another employee came in fifteen minutes late one day and her boss didn't mention it. She let it slide.

Another waiter noticed that the waiter didn't take very good care of the customer and no one cared. And another waiter noticed that people got to come in a little late and no one said anything. So that waiter decided that no one cared if you came in a little late so why bother to be there on time. Then someone else said, "If they don't expect good service from me, I'm not going to deliver good service as no one seems to care anyway."

Because the manager didn't mention it to the waitstaff, it became acceptable to be less than great at their jobs. Things started to slip in service, and it went from the waiter to the cooking staff to the busboys to the manager to the owner. Day by day, everything started to slide just a little. Five minutes here, five minutes there. Nothing all that noticeable or anything to get upset about right?

Why say thank-you to the customer? No one cares anyway. The customer didn't speak up or complain. The customer just accepted it all as the way things are in business today: crappy. And that's put the restaurant out of business.

Everybody let things slide because it just seemed petty to complain about any of those little bitty things until pretty soon people weren't going to that restaurant anymore, and before very long, that restaurant was no longer profitable. When it ceased being profitable, it had to close. A place that started out great closes in six months all because one waiter showed up five minutes late for work.

Is that how it really worked? It could have. Maybe. Probably. It works the same way in your business. If it wasn't one little thing it was another little thing. A little thing that wasn't big enough to mess with, bring up and correct. That's why you have to start thinking about things. What am you letting slide? What are you letting others get by with? What are letting yourself get by with? Ouch!

Business ethics is black-and-white. Same with personal ethics. You know whether something is right or wrong. You know whether you ought to do it or not. If you even have to ask if you should do something, you know that the answer is no.

You never question when something is the right thing to do. You never question it when something is the ethical thing for you to do. You only ask the question when it's the wrong thing to do.

You know I'm right about this. You've asked yourself the question before: "Should I do this?" If you have to ask then you know you shouldn't do it.

It comes down to ethics in the little things. Very few people are going to cheat and steal from the company in a big way. You're probably never going to do something to get you put in prison for what you do at work, but if you go to work and you make a couple of personal phone calls, you've still cheated and stolen from your employer.

You're a liar, you're a cheat, and you're a thief when you steal time or anything else from your employer. When you give less than your best or when you've performed in a way less than your very best, you've cheated your organization. You've stolen their money simple because they paid you for your best.

I take a hard line on this stuff and I would hope that you would too. You should remind yourself every single day that ethics is part of every move we make and every action we take. While you're at work, you do what you're paid to do. And if you have to ask if it's wrong, trust me, it's wrong.

It's About Your Uniqueness

I was asked a while back what the smartest thing was I'd ever said in my whole life. It didn't take me a second to answer. This is the smartest thing I've ever said: "Discover your uniqueness and learn to exploit it in the service of others, and you're guaranteed success, happiness, and prosperity."

Let me break it down for you. Discover your uniqueness. Let's say you own a business, and right next door there's a business that sells the same product you do at the very same price. You might say, "Larry, I don't have any uniqueness." Yes, you do. They don't have your exact location. They don't have your attitude. They don't have your employees. They don't have what you have to offer in terms of understanding the customer in the same way you do.

When it comes to product and price, you might be the same. But even with those things being equal, you still have a uniqueness that you must discover because you have something that sets you apart from who they are, something you can capitalize on and something you can *exploit*.

Although *exploitation* is sometimes considered a negative word, I'm saying to exploit your uniqueness in the service of other people. You get to serve people in a unique way. When you learn how to do that, you are guaranteed success, happiness, and prosperity.

3

Teamwork and Leadership Principles

'm going to start off with a statement that is going to shock you. Teamwork doesn't work.

I know, I know—you love your team. People love to talk about teams and teamwork and all that. Amazon has over 50,000 books that contain the words *team* or *teamwork* in the titles, but that doesn't mean that it works and here's why.

Teamwork doesn't work because someone on the team won't work. Someone won't do their part so the whole concept of the team doing the work falls apart. Normally you have one person who does the bulk of the job. You also have at least one person who didn't do a darn thing, yet they're the one to step up and accept all the credit, as if they had something to do with the achievement. That bothers me.

We walk through offices and see posters that say, "There's no I in *team*." Exactly. That's why it doesn't work. People are interested in the I. There's a T and E and an A and an M, but there's no I. That's why teamwork doesn't work.

I'm interested in what I do. I want the credit for my work. I don't want to have to share it with incompetent people who get mediocre results. I don't want to share my hard work with people who didn't do a darn thing. Aren't you the same way? It's ridiculous when people say that you shouldn't care who gets the credit. Total BS. Care. Would you say the same thing if we were to substitute the word 'blame' for credit? Would you care if you got the blame for someone else's mistake? No, you wouldn't. If you want the credit when it goes well that means that you should also be willing to take the blame when what you have done goes wrong. When we have a personal stake in the results we create better results.

Superstars

Chances are, if you're reading this, you're the kind of person who wants the credit. You don't play well with others either. You still have to work in groups of people, but you want to work with superstars. That's what we need: groups of superstars who share a common goal, and who all work together based on mutual respect in order to achieve that goal.

Superstars are the way to go, not team players. If you're hiring somebody, and in the interview process, they brag about what a team player they are, don't hire that person. You don't want team players working for you. They brag about how they can get along with anybody; they don't need any of the credit as long as the work gets done.

Do you want a person working for you that doesn't need any of the credit? How well do you think they're going to do their job? There's a reason they don't care who gets the credit: it's because they've never done work that was good enough to deserve it. That's why they don't care. They don't want to have to admit they're not a superstar.

They're like the ones who say, "I'm a people person." I don't want a people person working for me. I want a guy who puts her head down, places her nose to the grindstone, and gets stuff done. You do too. You want a superstar, a person who respects the other superstars and knows how to work with them to accomplish a common goal. Remember, it's all about accomplishing the common goal.

Superstars don't want to share any credit. None at all. That's OK. They shouldn't have to. After all, they did the work. Superstars get to write their own rules, and you know why? Because they get the results. They don't have to live by the same rules as the mediocre performers, because they don't have mediocre results. They have outstanding results, so they pretty much get to do whatever they please.

All people are not created equal when it comes to work or business. The people who do the most work—the superstars—get the most credit, the most money, the most privileges. That's how it ought to be.

If you're barely making quota, then your butt had better be in your chair early. You probably ought to skip lunch. You ought to let me leave before you leave every day so at least I'll think you're trying, but if you're at 300 percent of quota, I don't care if I ever see you. Just keep giving me those results. If you can do it from the house, if you can do it from the golf course, I don't care how you're doing it. You're at 300 percent of quota. That's how it ought to be.

Let me tell you another thing about superstars. They want to look good. You need to let them look good. Superstars don't like to play that old game of "hit the ball and drag Fred." It creates discontent. It creates resentment. A superstar wants to be out in front. They want to go at their pace, and as their leader, you ought to let them do that.

Let's say you're not a leader. You're not a manager. What does this even have to do with you? Let me tell you what it has to do with you. If you're the only person on your team, you need to be the superstar. It ought to be your goal to be the person who gets out in front, does amazing work, and isn't willing to share the spotlight. After all, you're the only guy on the team. Why should you have to share the spotlight?

You ought to be the person who gets the job done and becomes a superstar. If you do that, sooner or later you're going to have to add more people, and you're going to want to add more people like you. You want to surround yourself with superstar employees that have a common goal and are all about getting the right results, regardless of what it takes to get them. They do it ethically, with integrity, and with lots of hard work. That's what you want. That's the kind of person you need to be.

The Eight ATEs of Leadership

It's time to talk about leadership. This works whether you have a big group of employees, a small group of employees, or you are your only employee. Leadership principles work for everyone. They'll work in your family. You can build on them to run any kind of organization or group.

I hate acronyms and buzzwords, and I hate anything that's very cutesy, but this is one is so good I have to mention it.

I call these the Eight ATEs of Leadership. They're words that end in A-T-E. Isn't that cute? The Eight ATEs of Leadership. I could have had the Nine ATEs, but Eight ATEs just sounds better.

Let me give you these eight words and show how they will help you become a better leader in any area of your business or life.

CREATE

The first word is *create*. As a leader, you have to create three things: the *right environment*, the *right atmosphere*, and the *right group* of people.

When I talk about the right environment, I mean an environment that is physically conducive to getting the work done. Sit back, look at the place where you work, and ask, "Is this place clean? Is it inviting? Is it conducive to getting the job done?"

Then you create the right atmosphere. For me, this is a place where work happens. It's an attitude. It's a feeling that is pervasive throughout the entire organization.

Let me give you an example. Let's say you walk in the DMV. Does that place have an atmosphere that creates a feeling in you, the customer, of a place where work gets done? How about when you walk in the front door of the post office? Do you walk in with confidence, look around, and say, "Man, this is where work gets done. I'm going to be served well here today."

You don't get that feeling from either one of those places. That's because they didn't create the right environment, and they didn't create an atmosphere that builds confidence in the people who work there or in the people who go there to do business.

Your job as a leader is to create the kind of environment and atmosphere in which works get done.

Then you have to create the right group of people. It's tough, I will admit, because résumés don't always tell you the truth. Nor do references. Today you can't even legally say something about your former employees. You can't say whether they're an ax murderer or they were lazy, or they were amazing.

The best that you, the potential employer, can do is ask the questions that you legally can ask and trust your gut that this person is going to be the right one to hire. That's going to be a challenge for you, because some people are very good at being interviewed, but you can't always trust somebody's words. Some people are articulate incompetents. They talk a good game; they just can't deliver it. You know people like that. You've probably hired them. They talk a good game, but they can't deliver.

Let me discuss the right group of people. This is called the 20-60-20 principle. This is my unique principle. I believe this is how it works in any group of employees. Everybody that works for you falls into three categories. They're either in the top 20 percent, in the bottom 20 percent, or in the middle 60 percent.

The top 20 percent of your employees: we will call these the superstars. They are the cream of the crop. They get to work on time, they do their job, they have integrity, they're honest. These are the people you love to have working for you.

Then you have the bottom 20 percent. They are exactly the opposite of the top 20 percent. They're worthless to you, your organization, your customers, and their coworkers. They may be nice folks, but you didn't hire them to be nice. You hired them to get the work done, and frankly, they're not getting the work done. They don't get results.

That leaves you with the middle 60 percent. These people are pretty good at what they do. They're not all that terrific. They're certainly not superstars, but they're certainly not in the bottom 20 percent either.

Here's what I suggest. As to that top 20 percent, stay out of their way. They're going to get the job done whether you help them or not. It's in their DNA to do an amazing job. These are amazing people. It doesn't matter what their job is. They're the right kind of people. They have made the decision in their lives to be amazing, so they only deliver amazing work. That's the kind of person you want.

Understand this about the top 20 percent: they will leave you. They always do. They move on to bigger and better things. Your challenge is keeping them challenged. You have to figure out ways to keep them challenged; when you do that, your chances of holding on to them much longer is better. Even so, understand that the top 20 percent will eventually leave you.

Then let's look at the bottom 20 percent. These people don't contribute, they cost more than they're worth, so they ought to be fired. You say, "But, Larry, if I fire them, they might sue me."

Yes, they might sue you. That's why they make attorneys. Remember this: A good attorney is better than a bad employee, so get yourself a good attorney. Fight these people from the outside.

Don't let a bad employee ruin your organization. Don't let one bad employee tick off a customer. Don't let them treat your customers poorly. You can't afford to have bad employees in your company, so get rid of the bottom 20 percent.

Okay, so the bottom 20 percent is gone. The top 20 percent is up there working. Some of them will leave you. Now let me tell you what happens to the middle 60 percent. The minute they see an opening in the bottom 20 percent, they will slide down. You have people who have just been waiting for a chance to slide down to the bottom. The good news is that some of the 60 percent will move up into the top 20 percent the minute they see an opening. They've just been waiting for a chance too.

You'll always have a top 20 percent. You'll always have a bottom 20 percent. No matter how quickly you fire them, somebody will take their place.

Your role is to work with the 60 percent in the middle. That is your goal: teaching those people to move up to the top 20 percent. Your job as a leader is to move your middle 60 percent into the top 20 percent. Do what you can to make that happen.

This concept is going to save you time, money, and heartache, because it's going to let you look at your employee groups and decide where people fall. Then you can give them a chance to move up or to move down, so you can take action.

You take action on both ends, and you work with the people in the middle. That's the *create*. Create the right environment, create the right atmosphere, and create the right group of people.

COMMUNICATE

Then you move to *communicate*. The first thing you have to do is communicate the big picture. You go to each employee and communicate what their role in the big picture is.

A lot of people would do a better job if they understood what their role was. They don't understand the part they play in the overall success of the organization. Nobody ever sat down and explained to the janitor that they actually contribute to the profitability of the organization. The janitor probably just thinks their job is to keep the bathrooms clean, empty the trashcans, vacuum the floor, and mop the floors. They think that's their job.

That is not their job. Their job is to create a place that is conducive to more work being done and for customers to spend their money. That's probably never been explained to them. Every person in your organization, regardless of what they do, needs to have communicated to them exactly what role they play in the larger purpose.

EDUCATE

Then we move to *educate*. Train employees, of course, on how to do their jobs. We spend a lot more time correcting people for doing a poor job than we do teaching them how to do a good job. Train your people on how to do a good job, but also encourage them to spend time and money educating themselves.

Educate your employees. Show them what they should be reading. If you had an employee that knew how to manage their time, set priorities, and achieve goals in their personal life, would that employee be a better employee? Sure they would.

If you taught a person to have better organizational skills in their personal life and showed them that they could read this book, watch this video, or listen to this person talk about these subjects, would that translate to how they run their business and how they do their jobs? Of course it would.

Way too many employers think that all they're responsible for is educating employees on how to do their jobs. That's not true. It's the responsibility of the leader to help employees become better people in every area of life, knowing that when we build better people, we build better organizations.

Now this also applies to you as the leader. You have to practice what you preach. You have to be going to seminars and events and learning from audio and video and from reading books. You have to set the example.

Again, you're probably going to say, "But, Larry, there's just no time. I'm running the company." Of course there's time. You have to take the time to set the example. One way to do that is say, "Read a book." Then you walk in and say, "Hey, listen. I was reading is an amazing book. This book taught me this, this, and this. In fact, I'm going to give all of you this book," and pass out copies to them.

Share the knowledge. Give them skills so they can be better people and do a better job for you. One of the ways you do that is by giving them the knowledge that you want them to have.

DELEGATE

Next, *delegate*. You have to learn how to delegate, and this is how. This is really all you have to do. Just ask yourself a couple of questions: Can it be done cheaper? In other words, can someone at a lower pay grade do this? If they can, let them do it. And can it be done faster? You actually have people in your organization who can do things faster than others. It certainly can be done faster than you could do it. Let them do it if it can be done cheaper or faster or better.

Yep—you're the leader, you know it all, you're omnipotent. That's hardly the case. There are people who can do parts of your job better than you can. Let them. You also might find people who like doing certain parts of what you do more than you do. So, let them.

It's okay to delegate. You need to do what only you uniquely can do, and there are things about being a leader that only you uniquely can do. Delegate the rest. Get it off your plate. Let someone else do it for you.

PARTICIPATE

The next ATE is *participate*. Become actively involved in your organization. You can't sit around in your office and expect to know what's going on. It's been called a lot of things, including management by walking around, but the key is this: just get involved and participate.

I used to own a telecommunications company where I sold business telephone systems. I had people who worked for me installing these systems. I would be out with salespeople, and I would make commitments for getting a telephone system installed that my installation force could not meet. They couldn't because I didn't know everything it took to get the systems installed. I was putting them in a bind.

My installation manager came to me one day and said, "Larry, you're not aware of what it takes to get these systems installed. Come with us, so you'll understand before you commit next time."

So, I went out and learned what it took to get a telephone system installed. I didn't know how to do it, and I didn't need to, but I still needed to know what it took to get it done. After learning that, I never overcommitted again, because now I'd participated in the process and I understood what it actually took to get the job done.

You need to participate in the process as well. Get out of your chair as a leader, go out, walk around, and find out what's going on in your organization.

When you do, reward people for the good things and fix the things that aren't going well.

I'm a big believer in rewarding people, so let me give you a couple of keys to the process. First of all, do it immediately. When you see something being done right, stop, and reward that behavior right then. Don't do it at the next company meeting; do it then.

Then make the reward very specific to that person. You can't just pat people on the back and say, "You're doing a great job." That doesn't mean anything. Be much more specific. Say, "I like the way you handled that customer when you told them" whatever it was they told them. Be specific in your praise.

Praise publicly as well as privately. If you see behavior that needs to be rewarded, let that reward come out in a very public forum, so that person feels good. Here's something we see being done all the time; don't do it. Don't walk up to other employees and say, "Bill over there did a great job. Why don't you work as hard as Bill?" All you've done is demotivate them and tick them off at Bill. Now Bill doesn't feel good about the job he's done either.

Instead make the reward immediate, specific, and private. Then be careful about how you do it in public, and make sure no one is embarrassed or put down in the process.

That's how you reward people. It's not really all that hard. You reward people well when you're participating in the process and you see firsthand what's being done in your organization.

HIBERNATE

The next ATE is *hibernate*. OK, you've communicated what needs to be done, you've created the right kind of organization, you've participated in the process, you've educated your staff on what they ought to do, and you've delegated your tasks.

Now you're down to the place where you need to get out of everyone's way and let them do their jobs. An old line says, "Lead, follow, or get the hell out of the way." This is the "get the hell out of the way" part of the job. Let people do what you've trained them to do and go back and spend some time rejuvenating yourself. Besides, you've worked hard. You need a moment to yourself.

I spend a lot of time on airplanes, and I find that the instant the plane puts its wheels down, people pull out their cell phones, call back to their offices, and say, "What's going on? Has anything happened?"

That's not how you lead a company. If you can't even get off the airplane before you start calling, asking, "What's going on? What's going wrong? What's happened while I've been gone?" you haven't trained your people very well. You haven't trusted them. You haven't delegated. You haven't communicated. You haven't educated. You haven't done the things that I've talked about even enough to allow yourself to have a relaxed airplane ride.

Don't be that kind of leader. Don't think that you're staying on top of things by becoming overly involved. If you've educated, communicated, delegated, and taken all of the other steps that we've talked about, you don't have to be that kind of a leader.

EVALUATE

Then it comes down to *evaluate*. You've given your people a chance. You've done everything to teach them how to do the job. You've stepped back and gotten out of their way. Now it comes time for you to evaluate the job. You only evaluate two things: activity and productivity. That's it.

You never get to evaluate the person. You just get to evaluate the person's performance. So, stop evaluating people, and start evaluating your people's performance. Performance comes down to activity and productivity.

By now you already know that I'm not a big supporter of busywork. I am, however, even less a supporter of people standing around doing nothing. I like to see people working. In addition to judging employees' activity, you judge their productivity.

In other words, not only is the work getting done, but is the job getting done? Is the result being accomplished? Am I achieving the results that I need in order for the company to move forward? Those are the two things that go into results—activity and productivity—and they're what you have to evaluate in your employees.

Sometimes when we evaluate people, we walk up and say, "I'm going to offer you a little constructive criticism." That's a stupid concept. There's no such thing as constructive criticism. *Construct* means *to build up*; *criticize* means *to tear down*. You can't do both at the same time.

If you want to build people up, build them up. If you want to criticize their performance—remember, not the individual, but the performance—just stop and criticize. You're dealing with big boys and girls here—or you should be if you are a good manager or leader. They can handle it. They're grown persons.

You have every right to criticize a person's performance. After all, you're the leader. You're paying them to do the job, and if they're not, you certainly have the right to criticize their performance.

When you're evaluating people, think about *desire* versus *ability*. Does the employee have the desire to do the job? Does the employee have the ability to do the job? I've had lots of employees who were, on a scale of one to ten, tens in terms of desire. The problem was, they were twos in terms of ability. We have a lot of people who have the desire to do the job. They just don't have the ability. When you're faced with that, go back to that other ATE: educate people better so they have the ability to do their jobs.

It's comparatively easy to educate people to increase their ability. On the other hand, you have people who are tens in terms of ability and twos in terms of desire. It's hard to give somebody the desire to do better. I've had a lot of employees who were quite capable. They just didn't have the want-to. They didn't have the desire to do better.

AMPUTATE

That challenge leads me to the last ATE, which is *amputate*. Sometimes you have to cut people loose.

Sometimes you have employees that are absolutely ruining your organization, and you must cut them loose. I'm talking about firing them.

We think of firing in terms of something we do to someone. Firing is not something you do *to* someone. Firing is something you do *for* someone. Firing an employee actually does them good. It's for their benefit. You're releasing a person from a job where they don't fit, where they're not performing well, so they can find a job where they do fit and can perform well.

All of us want to work in situations, environments, and jobs where we can do our very best. If you have an employee who's not doing their best, it's because either they don't want to do well, or they can't. Help them do well, and if they want to, they'll be fine. If you have people who know how to do well but don't want to, let them go.

The old cliché says that one bad apple can spoil the whole barrel. The whole barrel can't fix the bad apple. Don't think you can fix an employee who doesn't want to do a good job.

If an employee really wants to do a good job, they will. If they're not, it's because either they can't, or they don't want to. If they don't want to, chances are they're never going to want to. In that case, you need to let them go and replace them with someone who does. The good news is that right now we have a workforce out there with lots of people who honestly want the job.

You don't have to have a bad employee, because bad employees hurt everyone. They are like a cancer on your business. They hurt the customer, and the customer is the last person you ever want to hurt. The customer keeps you in business and keeps you profitable. You need their money. Don't let a bad employee hurt the customer.

Bad employees also hurt other employees, because tolerating their performance sends a signal to all the other employees that it's okay to do poorly. It must be, because the boss hasn't said anything about it. (Remember my restaurant example?)

When you refuse to accept anything but stellar performance from everyone, you have a much better chance of receiving stellar performance from everyone. Don't accept bad behavior. Don't tolerate a bad employee, because it hurts other employees.

Most of all, a bad employee will hurt your credibility as a leader. Every employee in your organization knows who the heroes are and who the bozos are. When you're not spending time and effort getting rid of the people who are slacking off, it's destroying your credibility.

You do not want to destroy your credibility in front of the people who are actually doing the job. You will lose their respect, and as a leader, you need their respect. You will earn it by getting rid of the bad performers and rewarding the good ones. It's that simple.

Let's quickly get to the firing. First of all, it should never come as a surprise to any employee that you're about to fire them. They should have already been warned that their actions have consequences, so the consequence, the firing, should not come as a surprise. Things have led up to it.

If you're going to fire someone, you need to have someone with you who's taking good notes. You don't want to have it come back and bite you in the butt, and if you're going to have to bring in an attorney in at some point, you want good notes. Remember, the person with the most notes normally wins.

Don't ever argue with an employee about why it's being done. Again, they should not be surprised that they're being fired, so there's no time to argue at this point. State your case, do the deed, and walk them out the door.

Do it quickly. Don't drag it out. Don't say, "We're going to let you go today, and you have two weeks to hang around." Having them hang around will kill your business, because they will go around to everyone, and they can hurt you in ways you would not believe with your customers and your other employees. If you're going to fire someone, do it, and walk them out the door right then.

Those are the Eight ATEs of Leadership. You're probably saying, "But, Larry, you must have forgotten one. What happened to *motivate*?" As you've probably realized by now, I'm not a big believer in motivation. In fact, I don't think you can motivate anyone to go from one place to another, even to a better place.

I've trademarked myself as *The World's Only Irritational Speaker®,* so the best thing I can do is make you irritated with where you are so you can't wait to go to a better place. I want you to become irritated with where you are so you will do whatever it takes to be better. You will take any action. I want you to be so disgusted and disappointed in where you are that you will do something about it. As I told you at the beginning, my goal is to make you uncomfortable, to irritate you with your current results, so you'll be willing to do what it takes to get better results.

My goal as a leader in an organization is also to make my employees irritated with their current results to the point that they want better results. High achievers will love this idea, by the way. They will consider it a challenge. Others will look at you and say, "Your standards are too high. I don't want to work here." Perfect! That'll save you a lot of time. You won't have to fire them. They'll just go away, because they'll say, "This is a leader who has high expectations. I can't live up to those expectations, and I need to go to a place that expects less from me."

That's not about motivation. You can't motivate that person. It's about irritation. Become irritated with anything less than excellent. Become irritated with anything less than amazing.

Those are the Eight ATEs of Leadership. Remember this about leadership: we're not talking about managing the process; we're talking about leading people. There are no secrets to leading people. Get out in front. Give them something to follow. Set the example.

Follow these ATEs, and you will have *created* the right environment, the right atmosphere, and the right group of people. You will have *communicated* clearly what each person's job is and their role in the overall success of the organization. You'll have *educated* people, not only in how to do their jobs better, but in how to be better people. You will have given them life skills.

Then you've *delegated*. Remember, if it can be done faster, cheaper, better, or by someone who likes it more, delegate it.

You have *participated* because you're going to get out of your chair, and go around, and find out what's actually going on in your organization, and when you see the right thing being done, you will reward it.

After you've done those things, you're going to need to step back and let people do their jobs You're going to *hibernate* just a bit so you can plug yourself in and get juiced up so you'll have more energy for the next challenge. Learn to hibernate and let your people do their jobs.

Then you go back and *evaluate*. You evaluate activity, which will be obvious. You can tell whether a person's doing the job or not. Mostly you will be evaluating productivity, whether the job is actually getting done—in other words, results. If the job is not being done, you're going to cut that person loose. You're going to *amputate*. Get rid of the bad employees, and remember, firing is something you do *for* people, not *to* people. As for motivation, forget it. It's impossible.

Why Customer Service Is Terrible

Allow me to beat a dead horse: Customer service. I'm sick of talking about customer service and you are probably sick of hearing about and we are all sick of receiving it. And if that's the case, why are we still talking about it? There are so many books written about customer service, and you've probably listened to dozens of audio programs and watched dozens of speakers talk about it. So why are we still talking about it? I mean, seriously, why?

Let me tell you why: Because service sucks. Across the board, customer service is terrible. It's atrocious. Why? Complacency. No one cares. Employees don't care enough to do a good job. Their managers don't care enough to make sure they do a good job. It's pitiful that we're at this point where customers don't care enough to complain when someone does a bad job. You're going to have bad service as long as you're willing to accept it.

Do you remember the movie *Network* from 1976? Probably not but you should. Peter Finch won an Oscar, even though he was dead, for his character's famous line: "I'm mad as hell, and I'm not going to take it anymore." That's the solution to customer service. You have to refuse to take it. Stop putting up with it.

I refuse to accept bad service and so should you. Again, to quote my favorite person, Larry Winget: What you condone, you endorse. In other words, what you put up with, you endorse. Do you endorse bad service? No? Then why do you put up with it?

Not long ago I was out eating with some friends. Finally, the waiter walked up to us and said, "I'm telling you right now, I'm having a very bad day, so don't expect very good service. Now what can I get you?"

I was astounded that he had said that to me, so I turned and said, "I'll tell you what you can get us. You can get us a new waiter."

"No, I'm serious."

"Believe me, I'm serious too."

"But this is my table."

"That's where you're wrong. This is my table. I'm paying for this table. You're just paid to serve me while I use this table. You've already promised me bad service. I'm the kind of guy who refuses to pay for bad service when I've been warned of it in advance. If I agreed to accept bad service, that'd make me stupid, wouldn't it? Go get me another waiter."

Instead he left and came back with a manager. The manager asked, "Is there a problem?"

I told him the problem and said, "You know, I'm the kind of customer who just refuses to pay for bad service, especially when I've been warned of it in advance."

"Well, I guess I could get you another waiter, but you know, it is his table, and besides, he really is having a bad day."

Why, as the customer, is the quality of his day any of my business? Why do I care when I just want a good meal with good service? Why is it even the manager's business? Why do I need to know he's having a bad day, and why should I pay for bad service? Why should you pay for bad service?

Here's an even more important thing to think about. Why should your customers pay you for bad service? You know what? They shouldn't. No one should be expected to pay for bad service.

What does it take to fix it? It goes back to my number one rule in life and business: do what you said you would do, when you said you would do it, the way you said you would do it. That's all it takes. You do what you said you would do, when you said you would do it, the way you said you would do it.

Let me tell you what that means. Sometimes that statement is going to cost you money. Too bad. You do it anyway. Sometimes it's going to be embarrassing. Too bad. You do it anyway. Sometimes it's going to be inconvenient to do exactly what you said you were going to do, when you said you were going to do, the way you said you were going to do it. Too bad. I don't care how inconvenienced you are. The point is you gave your word. You move heaven and earth to make sure you live up to your word—without exception. No complaining. No whining. You do whatever it takes.

Customer service will never improve as long as we smile, grit our teeth, and take it. We have to complain. We have to make bad service known. But making it known to the person delivering the bad service won't help. They obviously don't care and that why you are getting the crappy service to begin with. We have to be willing to ask for the manager.

If you're not satisfied with what the manager has to say, you have to keep asking for the next manager. If you're not satisfied with what they have to say, ask for their boss. Remember, everybody has a boss. Keep asking for the next boss until you get an answer you're satisfied with or can at least live with.

Let me warn you that you will be known as a jerk. I'm known as a jerk to many. Surprise! I'm the guy who speaks up. Other people don't like it when you speak up. My family is sometimes embarrassed when I speak up. They've learned to live with it. They just kind of wander away so they don't have to witness it or be a part of it. Oh well, sometimes you are in this thing alone.

So, here's a word of advice for the company, who shall, from this point on, be known as the defendant. When I complain, say thank-you to me. Be grateful that I took the time to complain. Don't try to pass the buck. Don't try to lay blame else-where. If you're the one I'm complaining to, say thank-you. Suck it up and admit that a mistake has been made. Say you're sorry. Then do your best to make me happy. Present me with a solution. That's all I'm looking for.

Sometimes all I'm looking for is for somebody to say, "I'm sorry. We made a mistake. We'll try to do better next time." Just remember: This about *me*, the customer. My money keeps you in business. My money keeps your doors open. My money pays your salary. You had better be nice to me. You had better tell me the truth. You had better be there when you said you would be, with no excuses. You had better smile at me. You had better call me by name if it is at all possible. You had better be courteous.

You may have to kiss my butt a little, just as you might when the company president is talking to you, because you work for me. You need me, and like it or not, you have to have my money to stay in business, because no customer needs to do business with a company who continually delivers bad service. No customer will continue to share their money with a company that employs people who aren't nice to them.

Be nice and keep your ego in check. Don't get too full of yourself. Not even the world's best company, delivering the most unique product at a give-away price, can survive when they deliver poor customer service, because the consumer will gladly pay more for less when they are confident that they will be served well. I don't care what it costs. I want to be served well.

The economic condition of a company is the reflection of the service it provides. Look at how well you're doing. If you're not doing so well, chances are you're not providing amazing service. I'll put up with a poor product, I'll pay more for a poor product, but I won't tolerate bad service.

When you astound me with your service, you will be amazed at how much I will put up with in the other areas. And it's so easy to give amazing service. It really is. Just remember this: a deal is a deal.

When you and I agreed to do business together, we struck a deal, and the deal was you would make me happy with your product and your service. That's the deal. I'm your customer. Hold up your end of the deal by doing whatever it takes to keep me happy. It is your fiduciary obligation.

I like this line from Sam Walton, the founder of Walmart: "There's only one boss, the customer, and he can fire everybody in the company from the chairman on down simply by spending his money somewhere else." You need to remember that about your company and what you have to offer.

Delivering customer service really comes down to doing things that make sense. That's all we're looking for: we want things to make sense. When I'm out there as a customer, I don't see a lot of things that make sense. I'm going to tell you a couple of quick stories.

I was speaking at a convention. This one happened to be in Las Vegas. When I show up, I normally autograph books and offer some of my other products. I typically have a lot of stuff to sell with me and I always have these things delivered to the back of the room where I am speaking.

In this case, I had my manager and they were working with the bellman. We were all walking into the ballroom, where it was all going to be set up.

The problem was the bellman could only go to the door of the ballroom. He couldn't go all the way in to set down all of the boxes of product where the tables were. This was because the jurisdiction of the ballroom belonged to the decorators' union, and bellmen couldn't go in to actually set the boxes on the table, because it would be crossing into a different union's area.

I couldn't believe it. The bellman said the only choice was for him to leave all of the boxes in the hallway; then we could carry them into the ballroom ourselves. I said, "You're telling me that a union has decided you can't help a customer."

"I'm sorry, sir," I said, "but it is the policy that we cannot go into there."

"So, the union wins, and the customer loses."

"Yes, sir. That's exactly the way it works."

Now here's what's sad. The union thinks they won. They didn't win at all. They ticked off a customer who doesn't really blame the union but ends up blaming the hotel. I'll do my best to work at any hotel other than that one. So that hotel will lose money and that impacts profitability. And even though my business won't bankrupt the hotel, it matters.

Another story: I'm flying across the country. It's been a long day. I know that there's not going to be any food for Larry when I get to where I'm going. I know that at this particular hotel, room service stops at 11:00. I also know I won't get to that particular hotel until at least 11:30, so I'm stuck eating out of a machine that night, because there won't be any food. I haven't had a food flight all day long. I've missed connections. It's just been a tough day on the road.

When I get to the hotel, I'm standing at the front desk. At this particular hotel, when you check in, they give you a chocolate chip cookie. As I'm standing there at the front desk checking in, the front desk clerk hands me my chocolate chip cookie and says, "Sir, here is your warm chocolate chip cookie." I hug it to my breast. I cannot wait to get to my room to eat this chocolate chip cookie.

At the very same moment, there's a guy standing right next to me, checking in. His clerk hands him a cookie, but he says, "That's OK. I don't really want it. I don't like chocolate." (What kind of person doesn't like chocolate?) So, I immediately say, "I want that cookie."

His front desk clerk looks at me and says, "I can't do that. This cookie has been assigned to *his* room."

"Cookies have room assignments?"

The guy turns to me and says, "Hey, that's okay, buddy. I've got this. I'll hand it to you when I'm finished." He turns back to her and says, "Listen, I've changed my mind. I've decided I want that cookie."

She says to him, "I can't do that. The cookie has already been declined."

Does that bother you? It bothers me. That story happened to me ten years ago, and I'm still ticked off about that cookie. Little things like that make a big difference.

I could tell bad customer service stories all day long and you could too. Bad customer service is everywhere.

People ask me, "Don't you ever get any good service?" Of course, I do. In fact, I actually believe there's more good service being delivered every day than there is bad service, but here's the problem with good service: memories of good service don't last very long. I actually can't think of the last time I got such outstanding service that I've remembered every detail of it. Yes, I might have passed on the information to a buddy I was talking to. I might have said, "Yes, I got a great meal, or the service there was good," or whatever, but if you give me bad service, I can remember every detail. I know exactly what they said and how it made me feel. I know what action I will take as a result of it, and you're the very same way. We're all the same way.

We don't remember the good service long enough to tell too many people, but if you get bad service, you'll remember it forever. You're that way. What makes you think that your customers are any different? They aren't. Your customers will remember your bad service forever.

When you deliver bad service—and you will as we all do—stop, admit it, apologize for it, and offer a solution. Is it that hard? Take responsibility, apologize, and offer a solution. That's all your customer wants. Give them a chance. Make them happy by fixing what you've broken. It's not that hard.

Now there is such a thing as a bad customer. I'm about as pro-customer as anybody you'll ever find. I'm the guy who believes that the minute we do business, you work for me; I'm the boss. Nevertheless, I readily admit that there are bad customers.

If a customer is personally abusive to any employee, then in my opinion, that customer isn't worth having. Dump them. If a customer is just mean then you have to stop and ask yourself, "Is their business really worth it?" If it is, you suck it up and take it. But remember that you are choosing to deal with the abuse they're going to give you.

Some customers are not worth doing business with. These folks are going to beat you up all the time, personally and professionally. They're going to beat you up over price. They don't value your relationship and don't care about your service. They just want the best price. That's not a customer you really need.

My friend Mark Sanborn, author of *The Fred Factor*, has a maxim: "The customers who are willing to pay you the least will always demand the most." Decide in advance whether you're willing to compete on the sole basis of the lowest price. If that's the customer you want, then you have to understand that's probably not going to be your best, most loyal, most committed customer.

It all really boils down to this: we all do what we do for one reason and one reason only: to serve others well, knowing that the better we serve others, the better we are served in turn. That's what it comes down to. The better you serve your customer, the better your customer will serve you. Always commit to delivering excellent customer service.

While bad service has become the norm, the good news is that it takes very little to impress your customer. Go the extra mile. Do what it takes to please your customer. Move past your standard policies and procedures to make your commitment to customer service a personal one between you and the person spending their money with you and your company.

The customer has all the money. You need their money. The better you serve them, the more willing they will be to share their money with you. It's a universal law: The better you serve others, the better they will serve you.

Nothing Happens Until Somebody Sells Something

Red Motley, one of the original sales trainers of all time, said "Nothing happens until somebody sells something." That's true, and none of it is very complicated. In fact, let me show you how simple selling really is.

Let me ask you a question about your life: do you want to lose weight? Of course, you do. Who doesn't want to lose weight? It's really very simple. It comes down to two things: eat less, exercise more. You can fight me all day long on it, but I'll guarantee you it comes down to those two things: eat less, and exercise more.

Now let me move to business. Do you want your business to be more profitable? Of course, you do. It comes down to two things: reduce expenses and increase income. No other way around it. You either have to reduce expenses, or you have to increase income, or both.

You know how you increase income? You sell more. Simple as that. I'm not good at cutting expenses, so in my life and business, I've decided that the only way for me to survive and truly be happy and prosperous is to sell enough to support my lifestyle and my business.

In order to do that, I had to get really good at selling. My transition to becoming a professional salesperson was a natural one for me. I was born into it. My grandfather was a carny. He sold pony rides and tickets to see his monkey and his bear. That's what he did for a living. My parents both worked in retail for many years. I grew up around people who were selling stuff all the time. As a little boy, I picked strawberries from our huge strawberry patch and sold them door to door. I have been selling since I could walk.

Later I became a salesperson for Southwestern Bell. Then I owned my own company selling business telephone systems. For the last twenty-five years, I've been selling speeches. Along the way, I learned to sell books, tapes, CDs, DVDs, coffee mugs, shot glasses, bobble heads, online programs and more.

I know what it takes to sell things, and it's not as complicated as most people would have you believe. In fact, we've written all these books about how to become successful at selling, and it really comes to one very simple thing: *ask*.

That's right. Just ask. I'm not going to complicate it more than that. Ask people to buy. It's amazing what happens when you ask somebody to buy. Either they will say yes, or they will say no. If they say no, you ask them again. If they still say no, ask them again. If they say no a third time, ask them yet again. If they say no after that, move on. Ask somebody else.

But it still comes down to asking. What if you ask them, and they say yes? Then stop selling to them. The deal is done.

Ask people to buy. Don't be a pain in the butt about it. Don't ask people all the time. Many years ago, there was a sales program out called ABC, "Always Be Closing." People don't want to always be closed. They don't want you bothering them by asking them all the time.

You have to understand that selling well is about serving people well. I don't care what your product is. It probably makes somebody's life easier and more manageable. It saves them time and money.

Something about it helps people. If it helps people, it serves them. If it solves a problem that alleviates a pain, they will be served and gladly pay you for how you did it.

If you're selling people a product that helps them, you are serving them well. If you don't try to sell it to them, you're doing them a disservice. I believe you're actually hurting them. To have a product that helps people without asking them to buy it hurts them.

You are obligated to help others, to serve others well, by selling them your product based on the help, the service, the good things that it provides. Now is that simple? When you look at your product in that way, how could you *not* ask people to buy it? It's not that tough.

Just ask people to buy it. Ask with some common sense. Tie is back to the problem I am going through and the pain I am dealing with. When they get it, ask. You know when it's the right time to ask people. Ask with some tact. It's not that hard. Be nice. Be courteous. And ask.

Why is this stuff so hard? Why do we need all these books talking about the secrets of selling? Just ask people. It's not that hard.

Remember that people buy for their own reasons, they don't buy for yours. Before people shell out money, they need to have a reason. They won't shell it out until they have a reason, and the reason is not that you need to make the sale.

I've actually had a person tell me that he needed to make this sale because he was probably going to lose his job if he didn't. Do you think I bought from him? No. I don't care how hungry his family is. It's not my problem he's a bad salesperson about to lose his job. I didn't need to hear that.

Besides, I want to buy from successful salespeople. I want to walk into a business, look for their number one salesperson, and ask for them, because that person is number one for a reason: they're good at what they do.

People buy for their own reasons. Now this is very simple: find out what their reason is. Do you know how to find out why people buy? Again, simple. You just ask them. Ask what they're looking for. Ask what would be the 'one deciding factor'. This works so well, it's so slick that it ought to be illegal.

This is all you have to say: "I've discovered that people buy for one reason more than any other. Could you tell me what yours is?" They'll tell you, and when they do, you sell to that reason. It's not that hard. It really takes more time to figure out why people *don't* buy.

Why They Don't Buy

Now I'm going to give you the five reasons people don't buy. I wish I could take credit for this. I heard this somewhere many years ago, but again, I've read four thousand books, and I've listened to five thousand hours of audio and video, so I actually can't give credit to the source, but it made more sense to me than anything I've ever heard about this subject.

1. They don't have any need.
2. There's no hurry.
3. There's no money.
4. There's no want.
5. There's no trust.

People rarely buy what they need anyway. They buy what they want. Don't worry yourself with whether they need it or not.

There's no hurry. There's no sense of urgency. That's a challenge. You have to create a sense of urgency. You have to show them the benefits of making a decision now instead of later. It's always focused on creating a sense of urgency.

Next is no money. People will lie to you about this one. A lot of people do have money. They're just not willing to share it with you, because you haven't shown them yet a reason to, which moves you to the next one, which is want.

If you create a want or find out why they want it, people will spend money on it. They will obsess, they will lose sleep, they will lie, cheat, and steal to have it if they want it badly enough.

Your job is to make people want what you have to sell. Help them obsess. Help them smell it, taste it, dream about it, and lose sleep over it. When you do that, they'll move heaven and earth to get it.

The last one is the hard one: trust. People have to be able to trust you. You can't get a good deal from a bad guy. The fastest way for me to know you're a bad guy is a very simple thing, something I mentioned earlier. It's about being on time for your appointments. If you set an appointment with me, and you're supposed to be at my house at 2:00, you need to be at my house at 2:00. I don't care what problems you have. You need to be there at 2:00.

I recently did business with a fellow who set an appointment with me, and he said that he would be at my house at 11:00 a.m. At 1:30, he rang my doorbell and said, "Sorry, I'm running a little late."

"No," I said, "actually, you're two and a half hours late; we had an 11:00 appointment."

"Yeah, I got tied up this morning."

"Did you not have a phone? You couldn't call me? You couldn't let me know you were running late?"

"Well, I was busy."

"You know what? Your being busy cost you this sale, because I figure if you can't be on time to sell me what I'm trying to buy, then I doubt that you're going to be on time to deliver it, install it, or service it. Thank you very much for stopping by. I've already bought it from somebody else."

He was ticked off. Why? I don't understand why he was mad at me since he was the one who didn't keep the appointment. I'd even let him set the appointment.

Again, you're going to be known as a jerk if you do the stuff that I do, but the key is he didn't build trust. I lost trust in the quality of his product. I lost trust in whether he was going to be able to deliver it, set it up, and keep it working, all because he was late for an appointment.

Trust is the biggest challenge you're going to have. If people trust you, they will spend their money with you.

Let me give you some simple ideas on how to sell more. Don't get caught up in how simple they are.

Instead, just think about how you'll be able to use these ideas to sell more.

Number one: look successful. I like people who look successful. I want to buy from people who are successful. Success can be faked. I know it can. You can wear a good suit and drive a nice car and still not be successful, but it can't be faked for long.

Look great, dress well, drive the best car you can possibly afford to drive, and keep that car clean because your car is just like your desk, your office, and your building. That's the place where you do business. I need to be able to see that it's clean, so I'll know you're serious about your business and my business.

Next, be friendly but not overly friendly. If you're overly friendly or gregarious, if you invade my space, I'm going to think you're smarmy, and I'm not going to do business with you. You aren't my best buddy. Don't act as if you are. You're a professional there to provide me a service. Act like a professional, and be friendly with me, but not overly friendly.

Next, again it comes down to ask. The Bible said that you have not because you asked not. The Bible is right. Ask; just ask. Ask all the time.

Let's say that you work as a salesperson 220 days a year. That's a typical year. If, every single day, you ask just one more person to buy, that would be 220 more people you would ask. If you have a closing ratio of 10 percent, that's 22 more sales you're going to make. How much more money would that mean to you?

If you're on commission, 22 more sales would make a big difference, I bet. All because you asked one more person per day. Drive it down to the ridiculous. Ask people to buy. Ask everybody to buy, but don't be obnoxious about it.

Be observant. Pay attention to what people buy, how they buy, and when they buy. Observe your competitors. See how the other people in your business sell. Don't copy what they do, but learn from it. Be observant; pay attention.

Then listen to what your customer has to say. This is a tough one for most people. Most people are not good at listening. They think listening is just that time when you're quiet until you can start to talk again. That's not what it is. It's actually paying attention to the words of the other person so you can build on that in order to move closer to a sale. Listening is paying attention, which gives you the information so you can respond to what they have to say.

Next would be to know what you're talking about. Don't overpromise and underdeliver. If you say your product does something, then I expect your product to do what you said it would do. That's not too much to ask, is it?

Be able to deliver on what you said. Know what your product is capable of doing, when I can get the product, and what the product will do once I get it home. That's what your customer wants from you.

Here's a couple of other things you can do that will allow you to sell more. Be honest. Do I need to say that? I guess I do, because a lot of salespeople are not honest. Don't dance around when I ask you a question. Never lie to me. Don't try to mask the fact that you don't know what you're talking about. Just fess up. Tell me the truth. If you don't know the answer, tell me you don't know and go get the answer.

Return phone calls promptly, not days later with some feeble excuse. Again, be on time. You should be great on the telephone. When you're talking on the telephone, you don't have the benefit of being able to physically observe the other person. So, you have to be better on the telephone than you are face-to-face.

Give people good verbal cues. Grunt at them every once in a while to let them know you're listening and take good notes. Always work from documents, not from memory. You need to have the information written down. Actually, it's magic. Even on the phone, if you tell people you're going to take notes, they'll say smarter things. If people know you're writing it down, they will give you better information. They will be more succinct. They'll say it faster, and the information they give you will be more relevant to closing the sale. Take notes; let them see, or tell them, that you're taking notes.

Always deliver more than you promised. Never let a customer say, "I expected more." You don't want your customer to say that, so deliver more than you promise.

Once you've made the sale, follow up. It's not that hard. Just make a phone call, drop a postcard, say thank-you, stay in contact, because the easiest customer to sell your next product to is one you've already sold to. You've established trust, and you've proven that you're the kind of person that they can trust to share their money with.

There are some simple things, like having a great handshake. It's not a big deal, but a lot of people don't.

Capitalize on your successes. The best time to make another sale is when you're on the heels of your last great sale. Don't make a sale and then kick back and decide to rest on your laurels. That would be a big mistake. When you make a sale, capitalize on it by going after another one. In other words, when you're hot, you're hot. Go after the next sale.

Remember this when it comes to selling: You can't win them all. That's just the way it is. You need to be resilient. You need to have bounce-back ability. You need to know that even though you've had every door that you've knocked on slammed in our face today, tomorrow you have to go out and knock on more doors.

Sometimes you're going to lose. That's just the way it is. You don't need to sell them all. You just need to sell the next one, so keep looking for the next one.

You can have the best product and the best price in the whole world, but unless you're asking people to buy it, it won't do you any good. That old cliché, "Build a better mousetrap, and the world will beat a path to your door." Well, that's a load of crap. You have to beat a path to their door. You have to let people know how good your product is and what it will do for them. You have to ask them to buy, and it's not that complicated. Don't complicate this process. In fact, if you don't remember anything else I've said about selling, just remember this: Ask. Ask. Ask. That's all it comes down to and remember that people buy for very simple reasons.

Let me tell you a quick story. For years and years, I've gone to the same bank. I always go to the drive-in bank. I guess I went inside at some point to open up the account, but I honestly don't remember. I just go to the drive-in bank.

Years ago, I had my two little boys. They're grown men now with little boys of their own, but they were little boys then. Plus, I had my two dogs with me. We pulled up to the drive-in bank. Now when you pull up to the drive-in bank, you have a couple of options. You can go to the one that's up next to the building where the drawer comes out or you can go to the ones farther out that have little pneumatic tubes by which you send things back and forth. I prefer the one that's up next to the building. It gives a little more personal contact.

When I pull up in front of the window, the drawer comes out. The teller inside sees my two boys, sees my two dogs, pulls the drawer back in and sends it back out. It has two dog biscuits in it. I hand one to one dog and the other one to the other dog. Now my dogs are happy.

The drawer goes back in, comes back out, and it now has two suckers in it. I hand them to my boys. Now my boys are happy. I look back at the teller and ask, "What about me?"

"Well, what do you want?" she says.

I tell her, "I don't want a dog biscuit!" So, she sends out a sucker. I reach into the drawer, look at the sucker, put it back in the drawer, and send it back in.

"Sir, what is the problem?" she asks.

"The problem is that it's a green sucker." (Nobody really eats green suckers, by the way.)

"What kind of sucker do you want?"

"I want a red sucker."

So, the drawer comes back out with a red sucker in it, and now I'm happy. I leave the bank. My transaction is done. I come back about a week later. I'm all by myself. I pull up. There's a different teller, but the teller who'd helped me the week before is standing down the row, and you know how they can all stand and talk to one another. She waves at me. I have a new teller. The teller from the week before turns to the teller that's helping me now and says, "That guy right there—he likes red suckers." The new teller sends out a red sucker, and now a trend has developed. I've become known as the guy who likes red suckers.

This goes on for months and months. Every time I go to the bank, they send out a red sucker. I'm the guy who likes red suckers. I like having that reputation at my bank. Six months into this deal, I pull up. It's five minutes after 6:00 in the evening, and they're closed, but I can still see them all in there, so I wave, and they wave, and they shake their heads no.

So, I pull around front. The bank I go to has an ATM machine in the foyer with the all-glass front door right next to the ATM machine. The branch is so small that the tellers who help you at the drive-in window just turn around and face the inside counter, so they're the same people.

So here I am standing at the ATM machine in the foyer of the bank doing my transaction. I wave at everybody through the front door of the bank, which is all locked up. They all wave back at me. I'm doing my transaction when I hear the mail slot in the front door open up, and a little hand slides through the mail slot holding a red sucker.

I will never change banks. My wife and I bank at separate banks. That's just how we do it in our house. She has her account, her money; I have my accounts, my money. She said, "Larry, what kind of rates do you get your bank?" I'm not sure my bank has rates. They don't need to have rates. My bank has red suckers.

I will go to that bank forever simply because they sold me based on what's really important to me. Is a red sucker a good reason to do business with a bank? Of course, it is. I'm the customer, and I can't be wrong. At least not very often and not when it comes to red suckers!

In the next chapter, I'm going to talk about you and your money. I'm going to move you from wherever you are—whether you're flat broke or filthy rich—to a better place.

4

You and Your Money

t's time for us to talk about something that is near and dear to my heart, and I'm betting it's just as near and dear to yours: money. I like money, don't you? Money gives me great freedom. I get to do just about whatever I want. Why? Because I have money. If you don't have the kind of money that gives you the freedom to do whatever you want, you need to pay attention to this chapter.

I like to start off by telling people why I even have the right to talk about this subject. I didn't come from money. I grew up pretty much dirt-poor. When I was in the eighth grade, I made the decision that I was going to get rich. It was in eighth-grade civics class at Alice Robertson Junior High School, Muskogee, Oklahoma. I walked into class, and one of my buddies turned to me and said, "Winget, you only have one pair of jeans. You wear the same pair of jeans every single day."

I was busted because I only had one pair of jeans. He was right, but he humiliated me in front of a lot of people that I did not want to be humiliated in front of—a lot of girls. It bothered me, and it hurt my feelings.

I had no idea in the world what I was going to do, but I knew, right there at that instant, at Alice Robertson Junior High School, Muskogee, Oklahoma, that I was going to get rich. I didn't know how. I just knew I had to get rich.

And you know what? I did it. I got pretty rich. Then I made some really stupid mistakes. I lost it all, I went bankrupt and lost everything, but I learned from it. Then I went from rich to broke and back again. So, I'm writing from real-world experience. I've been broke. I've been rich. I know what it takes to go from one to the other.

If right now you're in a place where you're just getting by, you're deep in debt, or you have money problems of any kind, you need to pay attention to what I have to say. I'm a guy who grew up poor, lost all his money, and went bankrupt, and now I'm considered a leading expert on personal finance.

I used to have a television show called *Big Spender* on A&E where I talked to people in financial crisis. I go on major networks and talk to people about becoming more financially successful, having more money, and getting out of debt. I wrote a number one bestseller entitled, *You're Broke Because You Want To Be.*

So, I've got some experience with all of this money talk. No matter where you are in terms of money, I can show you how to get to a better place. That's what I'm going to talk about in the next two chapters.

I am not going to talk to you about investments; I don't really know much about them. I don't play the stock market. I don't do any of that stuff with my own money. I hire real experts, who have more money than I do, to invest my money in the stock market. I invest in things that I understand, and I don't understand the stock market, so I'm not going to talk to you about investments. Nor am I going to teach you how you can be your own stockbroker. The problem is—and this is the problem with everybody else who's out there telling you how to invest your own money—that even if we gave you the best advice in the world, you'll still never be anything more than an amateur investor. I don't want to trust my money to amateurs, so I trust my money to professionals who are worth even more than I am.

Besides, there are as many ways to get rich as there are rich people. You ask any rich people how to become rich, and they're all going to have different answers for you. I'm going to talk to you about how to get out of debt, how to move to a better place, and how to spend your money wisely so you can decide how to get rich your own way.

I'm not going to tell you any cute little parables. You ought to know by now that that just isn't my style. I'm not going to tell you that you ought to go live like a pauper. That's what a lot of people do. They love to talk about all those people who are millionaires, and we don't even know it. My goodness, look at how they live. They wear $70 watches and $40 shoes.

How much sense does that make? Where's the reward in that? Why would I want to work my butt off to become a millionaire and wear $40 shoes? I do not believe in living below your income level. I do believe in living comfortably within your income level. Don't spend more than you have, but it's OK to enjoy your money.

I'm also not going to talk to you about developing a prosperity consciousness or how to get beyond your poverty consciousness. I'm not going to tell you to touch yourself on the chest and affirm that you're wealthy. That just isn't my style. You can say, "I'm rich, I'm rich, I'm rich," until your face turns the color of money, but until you stop doing stupid stuff with your money and start doing smart stuff with it, you're going to stay broke.

Affirmations are fine, but affirmation without implementation is self-delusion. It takes work to be rich. I'm going to talk to you about the work it takes. I'm not going to tell you that there's a big secret to getting wealthy. There's no secret. It comes down to a couple of simple things.

Ask yourself these questions: Do you spend more money than you earn? Are you worried about how you're going to pay your bills? Are you barely getting by? Are you living paycheck to paycheck? Are your credit cards maxed out? Do you shop too much? Do you barely have any savings? Are you counting on your company retirement plan or Social Security as your retirement plan? Do you have more debt than you can afford to make payments on? Are you terrified of an emergency because if you had one, you would be left financially devastated? Are you clueless about how to fix your situation?

If you answered yes to any of these questions, you need to pay attention to what I have to say, because I'm going to discuss how to go from just getting by to getting way ahead, and it's not a complicated process.

Again, don't waste any time saying how much you want to get rich. I don't care how much you say you want to get rich, because you want your life to be exactly how it is. You're saying, "Uh-uh, Larry, you don't know me. How can you possibly say I want my life to be the way it is?"

Because if you wanted it to be another way, it would be. You have what you have because you want it to be that way. If you wanted it to be different, you would be doing something different. You're a person who barely scrapes by because that's the way you want it to be. You want to be a person who pays their bills late because you do. You want to be a person who buys things you can't afford because you do. You want to have a car that you can barely afford to pay for because it makes you feel better about yourself. That's why you do it. You want to wear the hottest new fashions instead of paying your rent. You know why? Because you do those things.

You want to eat out instead of saving for your kids' college education, because that's what you do. People do what they do because they want to do it. Period.

Do this little exercise for me. Quickly turn your head from side to side. Now when you did that, did you see anyone on either side of you holding a gun to your head, forcing you to do what you're doing? I'll bet you didn't. This means you're doing what you do because you want to do it. It's as simple as that. It's your choice.

You can get mad about it; you can say it's not fair for me to say that. I don't care. Your life is the way it is because that's how you want it to be. If you want to be broke, you're going to be broke. If you want to be in debt, you're going to be in debt, and if you want to be rich, you can be rich. Or you can at least be comfortably free of money worries. And folks, I don't care what amount you assign to that, that's rich.

What Money Will and Won't Do

You need to know how important money really is. Don't ever tell me money isn't important to you. That's a stupid thing to say. Money is really important. Money matters. In many ways, money defines you. I know that bothers people, but it's true. Money defines who you are because it defines your value in the marketplace and it defines the quality of the people, products and services you can spend your money on to fix your problems.

Money will determine the kind of school you go to or whether you go to school. Money will determine the friends you have. I'm sorry, but it's true. Money will even determine the kind of coffin you're buried in and what kind of gravestone you have. That's the way it is. Money defines everything in your life. It may not be fair, but that's how it is.

Money has defined your life up until now. Money determines what kind of doctor you go to. Money determines what kind of attorney you will be able to hire if you get in trouble. That's what life is about. Sorry, it's the truth. It's about the money.

The more you have, the better off you are; you can do a lot of good things with money. We're going to talk about what you can do with money, but never tell me money doesn't matter, because money always matters. Don't ever say anything stupid like, "Money isn't all that important to me," because I'll prove to you you're wrong. Money is important to you.

Admittedly we expect too much from money. We think it's actually going to bring us happiness. But people are happy if they want to be happy; money has nothing to do with it. Happy people are just happy people. Happiness is a choice. Let's not give money much credit when it comes to being happy or not happy. I can show you broke people who are really happy. I can show you rich people who are really happy. I can also show you a lot of rich people who are not happy, but I can tell you this: there may be rich people who are miserable, but they're miserable in a better part of town.

Money won't buy you any friends. In fact, a friend that money buys isn't much of a friend. Money won't solve your problems. More zeros does not mean fewer problems. Bad things happen to rich people just as they do to every other person on the planet. Bad things happen to everyone, but money will allow you to deal with those problems at a higher level.

Money doesn't even mean you're going to pay your bills on time. You're probably saying, "If I had all the money in the world, I could pay my bills on time." That's not the truth. People who pay their bills on time are the kind of people who pay their bills on time. They do it out of a sense of integrity, because it's the right thing to do. If people who have money are not the right kind of people, they're not going to pay their bills on time, whether they have lots of money or not. So, don't think that money is going to allow you to pay your bills on time. You will or you won't based on who you are, not what you have. It's up to you.

Money won't make you more charitable. Amazingly, people who have very modest incomes usually give a higher percentage of their incomes than people who have a lot of money. You're either a charitable person or you're not, so money won't do that for you.

Money also won't give you a better marriage. I'm sorry; it won't. I've worked with a lot of people when it comes to money. I worked with one couple who said, "Larry, really the only problem we have is money."

"Really?" I said. "Money is the only problem you have? You don't pay any of your bills on time, and you're about to be evicted from your home. It looks to me as if you have an integrity issue, because you don't pay your bills on time. That's not a matter of money, that's a matter of integrity."

They also told me that they had never really talked about their money problems, even though they had been together for ten years. Now these were people who had accounts in collections, and they were behind on their bills. They'd already had one car repossessed, they were about to be evicted, and they'd never really had a conversation about money.

"Well, then," I said, "it appears to me that you have a communication problem. Those problems are not money problems."

Rarely is money your problem, and it certainly won't give you a better relationship with your significant other. Money also won't make you successful. Success is about a whole lot more than just money. Success is all-inclusive. It's about having good relationships and fulfilling employment and being as healthy as you can possibly be. While money is not success, success does require some money.

Money won't make you a better person. If you're a bad person, you're a bad person. Good people pay their bills. They're charitable. They do the right things regardless of circumstances, whether anyone is watching or not. They work. They have integrity. They're honest. They honor their commitments and their obligations. They take responsibility for their words and their actions. They take care of their families. They do that whether they have money or not. Bad people don't do those things, and it doesn't matter whether they have money or not.

So, don't expect money to make you a better person. It won't. In fact, understand this about money: it magnifies everything. If you're a jerk when you're broke, money is only going to make you a bigger jerk.

If you're stupid when you don't have money, you'll just be more stupid when you get a lot of money.

Believe me, if the rich, young superstars of screen and music weren't rich, they'd still be acting stupid and crashing their cars, only they'd be doing it at Walmart instead of on Rodeo Drive in Beverly Hills. You just wouldn't hear about it. So, when you see rich people doing ignorant things, don't blame the money. Money doesn't make you stupid; it just gets your picture taken when you are being stupid so we can all laugh at you on social media.

I've spent a lot of time telling you what money won't do. So, what will money do? It will give you freedom. That's about it. It's going to give you the freedom to do what you want, when you want, the way you want. That's all money needs to do for you. That's all any of us want. We want the freedom to do what we want to do, the way we want to do, when we want to do it. That's what it comes down to. That's what money will do.

An Array of Excuses

You have excuses for why you don't have the amount of money you want. I know you do; everybody has. We all love our excuses. For some people, excuses are their best friend. You're probably saying, "I grew up poor." Big deal. So did I.

It's not how you start out that matters. It's how you end up. As I've already told you, my grandfather was a carny. He had a monkey, a pony ride, and a bear. He lived in a storeroom in the back of a furniture store. My folks never had very much, but I still figured out what it takes to be successful and do pretty darn well financially. You can do that too, so don't tell me how poor you are. You might be that way, but you don't absolutely have to stay that way.

Let me really step on some toes here. Don't ever say, "It's just God's will" that I be poor. What do you mean it's God's will? What kind of God do you worship who wants you to be broke? I've read books on nearly every one of the world's religions, and I have yet to find any of those gods who wants their people to have less than the best. What kind of God wants you to be poor? I'm not buying it.

I think God wants us to have all we can possibly have so we can help other people. I'm going to talk a lot about charity, because I believe in charity, and you need to have money to help people. They don't build hospitals with blank checks. You have to fill them in. You have to give some money to help people out.

I also don't want you to say anything like this: "I'm a single parent, and I work really hard, and it takes all I have when I get home just to fix dinner and watch a little TV, take a bath, and go to sleep." I know lots of people in this situation, and it's tough, but you can still overcome it.

I don't care how busy you are; I don't care what your circumstances are. I know people who are single moms, and they work two and three jobs in order to provide for their families and offer them some financial security.

Besides, do you know that the average American spends sixty-five days per year in front of the TV? If you added up all the hours, they would amount to sixty-five 24-hour days. Americans spend forty-one 24-hour days listening to the radio, seven days on the Internet, seven days reading the newspaper, and seven days listening to music.

You'd think that in all those days, they could find a little time to make themselves better at what they do and figure out a way to read a book, do some financial planning or get an extra job. So, don't tell me how busy you are and that there's no time. There's always enough time to do what it takes.

One of my sons is a fashion designer in Los Angeles, and he works about as hard as anybody that I've ever seen in his business. He works lots of hours every single day. The good thing is at least he can make his own clothes. He even learned how to survive in Los Angeles on $12 a week.

I've watched him go to trade shows, and while all of his peers were staying at Caesar's Palace in Las Vegas, he was down at the Howard Johnson's, paying $39 a night, sharing a room with his business partner, eating rice cakes, beef jerky, and candy bars, and drinking five for $1 sodas that he bought at the dollar store. He did what it takes. He paid his dues. He survived doing whatever it took to survive so he could eventually thrive.

Along the way, he learned how to speak Mandarin Chinese, Spanish, and a little bit of Japanese, so he could communicate with his suppliers and manufacturers. He wouldn't trade those days for anything. Now he's doing extremely well, and I'm very proud of him, but he worked hard and did what it took to be successful.

It didn't matter whether he had to lose sleep or do without food. He did what it took and worked as many hours as he needed to get the results that would finally pay off for him, and I admire him for it.

In any case, one of the people who work with him is named Joel. Joel moved to the United States from

Guatemala to make a better life for his family. He took jobs selling garments in large garment factories all over Los Angeles. He rode the bus an hour every single morning to start his job at 7:00 in the morning. He ended at 5:00, then he rode the bus back to his home so he could eat with his family of five kids, just to get on the bus again at 7:00 to go to the movie theater so he could pull tickets. He did that until 10:00 p.m. He then got on another bus to travel to my son Patrick's place, where he would sit at a sewing machine until 1:00 in the morning, helping Patrick sew samples. At that point Patrick would drive him home.

Joel did that six, sometimes even seven days a week. That's a lot of hours, but he never complained. My son said he never heard him complain one time. In fact, Joel was always happy, cheerful, and thankful just to be able to have three jobs so he could help his family go from getting by to getting ahead.

Now, Joel is a multimillionaire and employs many people. Did that happen by accident? Not a chance.

There are millions of stories like Joel's, so when somebody tells me that they're just too tired to do what it takes to take care of their family and provide them with financial security, I become very intolerant. You do what you have to do, and success takes lots of hard work.

Here's another excuse I often hear: "I deserve to spend my money the way I want." I believe you deserve peace of mind. I believe you deserve to have some financial security. From those two statements right there, I think more of you than you do. You think you deserve to spend the money any way you want to. After all, you earned it. I think you deserve to have peace of mind and financial security. I believe more in you than you believe in yourself.

Another popular excuse is, "I'm just too far behind, Larry. I'll never get ahead." I hear that a lot. "I'm so far behind, I have no choice." Of course, you have a choice. You aren't too far behind. It may be ugly for you, and things may get bleak, but you can always get farther ahead then you are right now.

I'm not going to insult you, though, by telling you it's going to be easy. It's not going to be easy. It's going to be hard. Remember, success requires hard work, but give yourself a little credit. You can get ahead. You can get out of the mess you're in if you're willing to do what it takes.

This is another popular excuse I hear: "I don't know how to get ahead, Larry. Nobody ever taught me." If you're fourteen, that'll fly with me. If you're thirty-five, it won't fly. It's not that hard to get yourself out of the bind you're in. You don't have to have a college degree in economics to get ahead financially.

All it takes is this: spend less than you earn. Pretty simple idea. Spend less than you earn. Invest a little money. Save a little money for a rainy day, because I guarantee you, a storm is on the way. You don't have to have a degree in finance to figure that out.

One guy told me he wasn't good at math. I said, "I'm not looking for advanced algebra here. I'm just saying write down how much you earn. Below that, write down how much you spend. Hopefully you'll end with a positive number at the bottom. If you subtract how much you spend from how much you earn, and you end up in the hole, you're doing something wrong. That doesn't require advanced math."

I've even had people tell me it was the credit card company's fault. Can you believe that? One person told me that if the credit card companies would stop sending her credit cards, she wouldn't be in debt.

Oh, my goodness. Can you believe somebody could actually say that? It's not the credit card company's fault. You don't have to sign that application and send it back in. Don't accept it. That's pretty simple.

Another popular one is, "Things just cost too much." No, they don't. Inspirational speaker Jim

Rohn says, "Things don't cost too much. You just can't afford them."

When I was broke, that statement meant a lot to me. Things don't cost too much; you just can't afford them. What's the solution? Earn some more money so you can afford whatever you want. It's not that hard.

I've also had people say, "Larry, it's easy for you to say. I don't make the kind of money you make. I'm not a doctor, a lawyer, or a ballplayer." I can show you lots of broke doctors, and I can show you lots of broke lawyers. There aren't many broke ballplayers, I'll give you that one, but it doesn't matter what you do for a living. There are rich janitors. There are multimillionaire secretaries. It doesn't matter what you do for a living. It's not about how much money you have. It's about what you do with the money you have, and we're going to talk about how to do smarter things with your money.

Last excuse: "I don't have any skills." Whose fault is that? Go get yourself some skills. You already can tell by now that I'm big on reading books. Read a book on what it takes to be successful. It's not that hard. Listen to some audio. There are lots of people out there telling you exactly what you ought to do to have more money. Pay attention to them.

That's going to take a little time, though—oh, yes, that's right; you don't have any time. Yeah, right. We all have enough time to do whatever is important to us. If being financially secure is important to you, you'll do what it takes to get that way.

You Know What It Takes

In fact, you already know exactly what it takes to be more successful. I promise you. You know exactly what it takes to be more successful and improve your results in every single area of life.

Let's say you want to be more successful in your business. I've already talked about that in the previous chapters. What could you do to be more successful in your business? I'll give you one suggestion. What if you just worked as hard as they paid you to work? Would you be more successful? OK, that's mine. Now you write down one. What's yours? What's your one thing you can do to be more successful at work?

How about being more successful with your family? Can you come up with one thing? How about this? "I'll stop parking my butt in front of the television, and I'll actually spend time talking to them." Would that give you a better family life? Of course, it would. OK, now what's your one?

How about your spouse? Do you know one thing you could do? I'll give you one. How about telling them that you appreciate them every day? Would you have a better relationship? Of course you would.

See, you can do this. Everybody knows what it takes to do better in their lives. You know what it takes to be a better parent. You know what you should do to weigh less and to be healthier. You know what it takes to become smarter. You know everything, and you know exactly what you ought to do with your finances too.

For instance, I'll give you one on your finances: only spend money on things you truly need. If you're broke, that's a good place to start. Stop spending money on things you don't need. Stop indulging yourself. Only spend money on things you need. Now you come up with one. You have one; we all do.

See, it's not hard. Everybody knows what it takes to be successful. The problem is that we don't do what we know. That's the problem. We don't take action on what we already know.

What's your excuse? You have one. You have a whole list of excuses. Whom do you want to blame? Do you want to blame your husband? Your wife?

"If my wife would just quit spending, I'd have more money." I've heard that. "If my husband didn't spend so much money on his motorcycle or playing golf, I'd have a whole lot more money."

You want to blame your boss? It's your boss's fault. He's the reason you don't have more money. You want to blame your parents? You want to blame where you live? You want to blame your ex-wife? You want to blame your environment? You want to blame your children?

I know. Let's blame the government. Let's blame taxes. Let's blame the weather. Let's blame your family or the company you work for or the fact that the housing market's in the dumpster. Blame whatever you want to. Write down all the excuses you want to, then go to the mirror, look yourself in the eye, and say, "This is all my fault."

That's what it comes down to every time in every situation: YOU. I don't care what you were left with or what problem you're facing, it's your fault. At least how you respond to it is your fault. No matter what your situation is in any area of your life, especially money, you can fix it. It can be better. I promise you, it can. I'm about to show you exactly what you need to do and what your real problem is when it comes to money.

Follow the Money

You don't have a money problem. Now you're probably saying, "I don't have any money. To me, that seems like a problem." Nonetheless, you don't have a money problem. It's the result of all your other problems.

You have problems with the way you think. You have problems with your attitude. You probably have self-esteem problems. You're probably lazy. (Oh, that hurt, didn't it?) You probably lack discipline. You lack integrity. You don't take responsibility. You don't have clear-cut goals, and here's your number one problem: your priorities are out of whack.

Your money problem is a result of all those other problems. Does that make sense? Let me prove it to you.

If you had clear-cut goals and clearly established priorities, and you spent your money on your priorities, you wouldn't have any money problems at all. In fact, life is a lot like a crime novel: if you want to know who the culprit is, all you have to do is follow the money.

I can follow the way you spend your money, and I'll know what your priorities are. Give me five minutes with your checkbook. Let me go through your credit card statement. Let me walk through your house, and it won't take me long to know exactly what is important to you.

If I walk through your house and every closet is full of designer clothes, then I'll know that's your priority. If I look through your checkbook, and you're spending way too much money at the mall, I know what's important to you. If I look at your credit card statement, and you're eating out every day, I know eating out is important to you.

Let me give you an example. I was talking to a guy who had a four-year-old son. I asked him, "Do you love your son?"

"Of course, I love my son."

"I have to disagree with you," I said. Believe me, you get somebody's attention when you tell them they don't really love their son. "You smoke three packs of cigarettes a day. That's $15 a day. You don't spend $15 on your son every single day. You haven't put aside $15 to make sure your son has a financially secure future. You're about to have your car repossessed, and you're about to be evicted from your apartment. You don't even work full-time, and you tell me you love your son, but your actions show me something totally different. Your actions show me that you love yourself and your cigarettes more than you love your son."

That did not make him a happy guy. He didn't have many nice things to say to me, but was I right? It didn't matter what he said. I looked at what he did, and what he did was spend money on himself. He spent money on his priorities. The money showed me that what was most important to him was self-indulgence, regardless of what he said about his son.

I worked with him. I convinced him to quit smoking. He got a job. He started saving for his son's financial security. I caught him up on his bills. In the long run, he realized I was right.

So, look at where you spend your money. Go through your checkbook and look at your credit card statement. Make a list right now of how you spend your money. Just look at the last month. I don't want to embarrass you too much.

Figure out how much money went to shopping, how much money went to eating out, how much money went to things above and beyond the things that were really important, like food, rent, paying your bills, and saving and investing. I'll bet you're going to realize that your priorities are out of whack.

This is an easy thing to fix. It really is. All you have to do is establish new priorities. Determine what's really important to you, and watch your

money go toward the things that are really important to you.

What's Important to You?

What is important to you? Take a sheet of paper and
make a list. It won't take you long. You know what's
important. I can help you fill it in.

Set aside the things that you say are important
and write down what's really important. I'll bet you
what's important to you is financial security for your
family. I'll bet you want to live in a nice home that
you can easily afford. I'll bet that you want to have
your bills paid. I'll bet you want to drive a nice, reliable car. I'll bet you want to have the freedom that
comes from having enough money.

If those things are on your list, that's where your
money needs to go, not towards the things that give
temporary satisfaction. Those things don't bring you
long-term happiness, so make sure that you know
what's important to you and funnel your money in
that direction.

Again, I don't want you to concern yourself with
how you're going to do these things. How you get
rich doesn't really matter. It's *why* you want to get
rich. That's what really matters.

When I was in the eighth grade and I decided I had to get rich, my *why* was that I was never going to experience that humiliation again. I refused to feel that way ever again. I would never feel poor and broke. That was my *why*. That motivated me along the way.

You need to know why you want to do this. You want to do it because you love your family. I know you do, so make that your why if you want to.

I stand in front of a lot of people. I have a lot of books out there, and a lot of people have heard me on stage and seen me on television, so they feel free to write me about their problems and want to know what I think they ought to do to fix their problems. I get a lot of letters, and recently I got one that really bothered me.

The writer stated that he was thirty-six years old, he had a job as a mortgage broker, he had three children, a loving wife, and a dog, but he had lost his motivation to succeed. He said, "Larry, I've lost my motivation to succeed. Could you please help me get my motivation back?"

I wrote him back and told him, "Your letter makes me sick. You wake up every morning and have three little babies in that house. You have a loving wife. You even have a dog. What more motivation do you need to succeed? That's your motivation."

I've already mentioned my father, who worked for Sears for forty-seven years. He never concerned himself with his motivation. He did what he had to do because he had obligations. He had bills to pay. He had a family. He had two kids to take care of. He did it without question because he had to do it.

That's what we have to be reminded of. We do what we have to do because it's the right thing to do, not only for our families but for ourselves. Don't ever tell me you don't have the motivation to succeed. Don't tell me you don't have a good reason to get rich. The reason you ought to get rich is that you can. The reason you ought to pay your bills on time and get out of debt is that you can, but it has to be important to you.

You need a strong *why*. Again, I don't care about *how* you're going to do it. I care that you have a strong why to do it. When you've identified why it's important to you, you'll figure out how.

Know Where You Are

All right. Now you've decided you want to be rich and you have a strong why. What do you need to do? Here's the first step: know where you are. You would be amazed at how many people don't have a clue to how much money they really earn.

Do you? Do you know how much money you earn after taxes? Do you know exactly how much money you have on hand? Do you know how much money is in the bank, how much you have in savings? If you know exactly how much money you have to work with, then you're ahead of most people.

Write down that number. It's not that hard. Write down how much money you have, how much you earn on a regular basis, and how many times per year you earn it, whether it's once a month, twice a month, or biweekly, which would be twenty-six times in a year. Figure out how much money you have to work with. Know where you are.

Then figure out exactly whom you owe money to. Believe it or not, people often don't know whom they owe money to. Some don't have a clue at all. I have worked with people when after doing some work on their money and going through all of their bills and debts, found they were spending as much as $7,000 a month more than they earned. That's insane! How were they doing it? They were doing it on credit. They were doing it by not staying current on bills. They were falling farther and farther behind every single month and didn't even understand until they wrote it all of this stuff down. Just like I am asking you to do.

So first write down how much you have to work with. Then write down whom you owe money to and how much. Then—this is simple—I want you to figure out whether you have enough money to pay the people you owe. If you do, get to paying them, and if you don't, you have some work to do.

If the number at the bottom is bigger than the number at the top, you have a problem, and the problem is that you're spending more than you make. That's where things have to change.

If you are spending more than you make, here's what you need to do: feel really bad. That's right. I want you to feel really, really bad. Those motivational guys won't tell you this. They want you to have a pie-in-the-sky, rose-colored-glasses attitude, no matter what your situation is. They're wrong.

I want you to feel like crap. I want you to experience real remorse. I want wailing and gnashing of teeth of biblical proportions. I want you to go to the mirror, look yourself in the eye and say, "Oh, how could I be this stupid?" You need to have a Jimmy Swaggart moment here. Remember Jimmy bawling his eyes out on TV wailing, "Lord, I have sinned!!" You need a moment like that. You need to beg forgiveness. You need to say, "What have I done? I've ruined my life. I've ruined my family's life." And you know what? You have. Feel bad about it. Take a little time to feel like crap, because you've made some horrible mistakes and you deserve to feel bad.

It's the people who feel the worst who usually make the most progress. I've dealt with people who say, "Yeah, it looks to me like I spend too much money" and laugh about it. You know what? They're not going to change.

Then there are the people who come to me and say, "Holy crap, Larry, what have I done? How am I ever going to fix this?" When they tie emotion to their stupidity and feel really bad and apologize to the ones they hurt, their chances of fixing things get much better. Those are the people who make the biggest progress. They feel bad enough and experience enough remorse to actually make changes in their lives.

I don't think you can really make a change unless you experience some remorse. I'm a big believer in pain as a motivator. I don't think I can say, "The grass is greener over there" and you really should go over there and then have you do it. But if I can make you feel some pain, the more the better with where you are, you might be willing to do what it takes to go over there.

Okay, so now you've wallowed in your mess. You've come clean to everybody in your family, apologized for being stupid and cried. Now get over it and get after it. You don't get to wallow in your crap very long.

Now it's time for the solution. You get just a few minutes to feel bad, and then it's time to go to work.

Time to Go to Work

What do you do when you want to go to work? First of all, I believe we live backwards. We figure out how much money we have, and then we spend it as best we can, and we live and enjoy ourselves on what's left over. I think that instead, you should determine exactly how you want your life to look and figure out how to make enough money to support that lifestyle. In other words, go back to the sheets of paper. (I'm big on lists, especially when it comes to money. Again, work from documents, not from thoughts or imagination.)

Get a sheet of paper and write down how much money you want to earn. Don't know? Okay, save that one for last. Instead, figure out how much money you'd like to have in savings. Give yourself a number.

How much money would you like to be able to give away? Yes, you have to give away some money. Sorry, that's your obligation. When you have money, you have to give it away, so write down how much money you want to give to charity.

How much money would you like to have in an education account for your family, for your kids? How much money would you like to have in an emergency fund in case something happens? Because, believe it not, something's probably going to happen, and you're going to need some money.

How would you like to dress? Where would you like to shop? Where would you like to travel if you could travel anywhere and money we not an issue? What restaurants do you want to eat at? What kind of car do you want to drive? What would you like to own that would just make you feel good and that you could have fun with? What kind of house do you want to live in? What part of town? Which town would you like to live in?

These are the kind of questions I want you to ask yourself. I'm not going to give you all of them, but right now sit down, dream about what you'd like your life to look like, and then determine how much money it's going to take for you to live that way.

I bet you've never done this before. Again, you're living backwards. You're living on what's left over. You're shopping on what money you can afford to shop on. You're eating at places that you think you can afford to eat at. Instead, do it backwards. Sit down, dream big, and then figure out how much money it's going to take for you to live that way.

Then go about figuring out how you're going to earn that much money and remember this: You don't *make* money. You're not the mint. You *earn* money.

How do you earn money? I've already devoted three chapters to telling you what it takes. Work. Work hard on yourself. Work hard at your job. Work hard at serving others well, knowing that the better you serve them, the better they serve you. Provide value to others. Become invaluable. That's how you earn money.

When you've earned the amount of money that you want, you can live any way you want to. See how simple this plan really is?

Five Stories

At this point, you may think that this is absolutely overwhelming and that there's no way in the world you can go from where you are to a better place.

"You have no idea what I've been going through, Larry. You just don't understand. I don't think I can make it."

Let me tell you that you can make it. I have proof that it can be done, regardless of where you start out. I want to tell you five stories about my friends. These are personal buddies of mine; I picked up the phone and called to ask them how they made their money, what their background was, and what were their keys to becoming multimillionaires.

These were regular people. Not one of them started out with any money. They all started out from very humble beginnings. They've all been broke, they've all been desperate, and they've all been scared to death about how they were going to survive financially, but they did it.

JOE

First of all, let me tell you about my friend Joe. Joe is a professional speaker, author, entrepreneur, restaurateur, and real estate investor. Like me, he grew up dirt-poor and now is one of the most successful business consultants and speakers in the country.

He grew up on a little dairy and tobacco farm down in Tennessee. He tells me that he was poor and that he didn't even know it. He wore clothes that were handed down from his big brothers. His mama bought groceries according to what was on sale that day. His family never took a vacation.

But Joe was interested in books. He got interested in the James Bond books by Ian Fleming. To Joe, it wasn't about the spy stuff, it was the fact that Bond was going to amazing places and a living a high-class lifestyle. Joe liked reading about Nassau, Paris, Monte Carlo, New York City, and all those places.

Joe became fascinated with that lifestyle. When he was in high school, he would skip classes and drive to Nashville, about thirty miles from his home, just so he could drive around in the richest neighborhoods in the city. Here he was, a sixteen-year-old kid with absolutely nothing, from a little bitty country town, and he was cutting class so he could look at big, expensive houses.

But even more than houses, travel, and all of the other things, to Joe money represented freedom from worry. He had spent his life watching his parents worry about money every single day, and he didn't want to live like that.

Joe went to college. He got a degree in political science. He took a lot of different jobs. He booked bands in nightclubs. Eventually he became a real estate agent, which was amazing, since he loved driving around those amazing houses. Here's the other amazing thing: he hated selling houses.

One day Joe went to a seminar and heard Tom Hopkins, at that time one of the biggest names in real estate training and professional speaking. As he watched him, Joe decided that that was what he really wanted to do for a living: travel around the country, doing seminars; he thought it would be a great time. At that moment he decided that that was what he would do at some point.

It took Joe a long time to make that move, but eventually he did, and he became a small business owner. He was his own business. He became a speaker and trainer. He knocked on lots of different doors trying to figure out how to sell training of any type to anyone in any kind of business.

Like most new small-business owners, he was so busy trying to live on the little money that he did make that he didn't save anything for taxes. Believe me, I've been there. Maybe you're there right now. In fact, as he puts it, at the end of the year, he would find himself on the floor in a fetal position, facing a tax bill that there was no way he could pay, but somehow he stuck with it. That's the key.

He was persistent. In fact, he said persistence is one of the main keys at being successful, along with education. Joe read everything he could put his hands on. He read business books; he still does. He reads *The Wall Street Journal*, *Architectural Digest*, *The Economist*, all the fashion and music magazines. He read every newspaper he could lay his hands on. He became a voracious reader so that he could get all the information that he possibly could. When you combine education and persistence, there's no way you can be beat.

Lastly, Joe told me that he never once had a written business plan, but he did have goals. In other words, he knew exactly what he wanted his life to look like, and he stuck with it until that was exactly what it did look like.

As I said, Joe is now one of the most highly paid and successful business consultants in the country. He regularly travels to the places he read about in James Bond novels, and he lives in one of those big, expensive houses, just like the ones he drove by when he was cutting class in high school.

JOHN

Now I want to tell you about John. John is an insurance agent and financial planner in Fort Worth, Texas. John grew up poor. His daddy installed drywall during the week and preached on Sundays, and he refused to take any pay for doing that. According to John, his family seemed to mistake being financially downtrodden for righteousness. Although they didn't really know any rich people, they could only assume that rich people were sinful. His family's biggest financial extravagance was sometimes, once a month, to go out to a hamburger joint for a hamburger. In fact, he never had a steak until he was in college. John's family just didn't have much when he was growing up.

He worked every day after school with his father to learn the trade of installing drywall. He was a journeyman drywall installer by the time he was fourteen and as good as any grown-up man on the crew. Around this time, his family went through one of their many financial crises. At that point John promised his mother that someday he would be rich so she would never have to worry about money again.

He said that it wasn't a flippant comment at all. It was a promise that he resolved to make happen. John says of all the promises he's ever made to anybody, this one to his mother has been the most rewarding to him.

So, John worked installing drywall all the way through college. He said it amazed him that people would work so hard by the hour without having any interest in how the business worked. They just wanted their pay for the hours they put in, but John wanted to understand business well enough to get rich.

John was a music major and never really had any formal business training. He never took business math in college, but it all just seemed pretty simple to him. As he told me, "If I got paid $200 for a day's worth of work and I owed my helpers $100, then I was a businessman. On the other hand, if I got paid $100 for a day's work, but owed my helpers $200, then I was a fugitive, because if I didn't have the money to pay them, they'd probably kill me with their tools."

A pretty simple idea, and it worked for John, so he set certain financial targets. If he met them, he would reward himself with a steak dinner at a nice restaurant. Before too long, John was eating steak every single night.

John says the simple math of being wealthy makes great sense to him. If you're broke then the cost of a hamburger seems very high. If you have tons of dough, then the cost of that very same hamburger seems pretty insignificant. John set a goal that he was going to work so hard and make so much money that the cost of everything he wanted in his life would seem insignificant to him.

John decided to study all the ins and outs of money and prosperity. He decided to learn all he possibly could about how to obtain wealth and invest it wisely.

Now John is a financial planner specializing in older Americans whose net worth is in excess of $100 million. He is fascinated by the commonalities he's discovered from working with wealthy people. In fact, he said it comes down to a handful of very simple things: competency. As I said, you have to be good at what you do. Hard work, perseverance, serving others according to their needs and not your own, and then always spending less than you make.

BRAD

Next there's Brad. Brad coaches and leads one of the top financial planning offices for a major firm in Canada. Brad grew up in a house full of people: two siblings, a single mother, an aunt suffering from MS, plus a grandmother and a grandfather, all living in one tiny house with one bathroom. Brad's bedroom was a closet off the living room. According to him, love was plentiful, but money was always tight. They felt it most on Thursday nights. That was grocery shopping night and going to the store was always full of tension and stress because there wasn't enough money to get what they needed and certainly not enough to get what they wanted. It was always day-old bread, powdered milk, and orange crystals instead of real orange juice.

Those experiences made Brad hate the feeling of not having money. The defining moment was when he decided to stage his own personal hunger strike before Christmas. He thought in his mind that if he didn't eat, it would save his family money so they could have more for Christmas. After three days of not eating, he just couldn't go on. He decided that money was not going to dictate his life; rather, his life was going to dictate his money.

Brad decided to become rich. He worked in construction and lived above a funeral home for $100 a month rent. He moved on to retail so he could make a few more bucks to live on and so he could buy books. Buying books was the key for Brad. He made success and wealth a study course, and he read at least fifty books a year.

Looking back, Brad said he spent way over $100,000 at Brad's University of Wisdom by investing in books and attending seminars. Even after becoming a multimillionaire, Brad still attends lectures and seminars all over the world and listens to some of the greatest thinkers and leaders of all time.

Brad began surrounding himself with like-minded people, who would challenge him and force him to become better. Brad has kept a daily journal for twenty-five years. You give him a date, and he can go back to his journals and flip right to that date and tell you what he was reading and what he learned that day.

In fact, when I was writing my book *It's Called Work for a Reason,* I wanted to ask Brad about something I knew I had said in a seminar years before, so I called him. He went back to his journals, and ten years before that time, he had notes from the speech that he had heard me give. He gave me exactly what I was looking for. I was amazed. Brad loves his journals and constantly reviews them to remind himself of all the great things that he's learned. What a great source of information your journals can be.

Brad is also a voracious goal setter. In fact, every New Year's Day, he sits by the pool in some beautiful resort somewhere around the world and makes a list of everything he wants in all areas of life. These things include money goals, spiritual goals, business goals, personal goals, goals for travel, family, and anything else that comes to his mind. He writes these things down, and they are specific. He makes his family do the same thing. He puts his kids through the same process.

If you had asked Brad when he was a teenager what he wanted his life to look like today, he says, "It would look just like it does right this minute." He's always known what he wanted his life to look like. He wrote it down. He set a plan to make that happen, and he did. In fact, he said his dreams are so precise that he could draw an artist's sketch of all of them.

Brad right now lives like a movie star with the anonymity of a regular guy. He loves life, family, and friends, and he laughs in the face of all the people who told him it would never happen for him.

PEGGY

Next there's Peggy. Peggy is a real estate agent and developer. She was born into a poor family. She describes her father as a mean alcoholic, but when he was sober, she was able to draw great self-confidence from him.

As a child, people would ask her, "What do you want to be when you grow up?" She would spell out things like actress, airline stewardess, mother, dancer, veterinarian, scientist, archaeologist, and all the other things that interested her at the time.

Most people, when they would hear her say that, would say, "Oh, you just have to pick one," but her father told her she could be whatever she wanted to be, and amazingly, she believed him.

At the point when Peggy was twelve years old, she began to blossom, and her family didn't have enough money to keep her in bras. She was humiliated. She said, "This will never happen to me again." Remember, my motivation was a pair of blue jeans. In Peggy's case, her motivation was a bra.

Peggy graduated from high school in May and got married in July, at the age of eighteen. Her first son was born six days after her nineteenth birthday. Within five years, she had two more sons. At the age of twenty-six, she found herself getting divorced from a man who promised that if she left him, he would never pay her any child support, and he kept his word.

Peggy had never worked outside the home, and she had no skills of any kind other than typing, which she had learned in high school. She rented an old typewriter, started practicing her typing skills, and landed a job as a legal secretary.

After a week, the law firm figured out that her skills were very limited, and they fired her with two weeks' pay, but Peggy remembered thinking, "That was really pretty easy. I'll just go out and do it again," so she did. The next job she landed paid $470 a month gross income. Here she was with no child support to help her, and her rent was $350 a month. To make ends meet, she sold everything she owned.

A man she started dating at the time taught her how to deal poker, so she landed a job dealing poker at night and working as a secretary during the day but working two full-time jobs while you try to raise three small boys was tough. As she puts it, "Those were dark days," but she says she is grateful for the gift of desperation, because that's when she made up her mind to survive, and she did.

Peggy needed to find something that allowed her more flexibility with her schedule, so she started selling real estate. When she first began selling real estate, she had been able to save only two months' worth of living expenses, and because she was on only straight commission, she had to sell something fast. Her first commission, on a house that was worth $19,000, was a little over $500, which she had to split with her broker. A year later, she bought her own house, which was pretty good for a girl who only two years before had never even owned a car.

Peggy now does what she does not to survive but to help people's dreams come true. She has a love affair with selling real estate, and she's come a long way since that first commission check of just over $500. Now her average commission is over $20,000. She owns dozens of houses, and she regularly buys, renovates, and sells houses in addition to her regular real estate endeavors. She and her associates are rated the top team in her market, and she has a net worth of almost $3 million. Peggy's story is an inspiration to all.

RANDY

Last is the story of my friend, Randy. Randy is an entrepreneur, author, multimillionaire, and most of all a world traveler, who does whatever he wants whenever he wants.

Randy grew up poor. He was the middle child of a single mother who raised three kids while knocking on doors selling Avon. Randy began with nothing but a determination to improve himself. The most important factor for Randy was making the decision to be wealthy.

Even as a child, Randy hated being poor and swore that someday, somehow, he would become rich. He told all of his friends that he would be a millionaire by the time he was thirty-five years old. Guess what year he made it. It was in the year he turned thirty-five, which is amazing when you consider that Randy was a teenage alcoholic and then moved right on to hard drugs.

Randy was expelled from high school at the age of fifteen. Then he went to jail for a series of burglaries and armed robberies. Yet even in those troubled times, he had a belief that somehow he could turn his life around and become wealthy.

It'd be nice to say that Randy figured out what to do as soon as turned from a life of crime, but that's not the case. Even though he dedicated himself to hard work, things didn't change quickly for him. He didn't have any clearly defined dreams. He knew what he was running away from, but he didn't have a clue about what he was running to.

Randy fell prey to the common belief that money is bad, rich people are evil, and somehow it's noble or spiritual to be poor. He started working hard on lots of different jobs and started opening different businesses. He opened up a restaurant, but it didn't work for him. Nothing seemed to work for him.

Randy finally reached the breaking point when his business was seized by the tax authorities and auctioned off for debt. Here he was with no car, no money, no credit cards, and $55,000 in debt. He sold his furniture to pay the rent and slept on the floor.

Randy's life sucked, but he stuck with it, because by this time, he had started to develop a vision for what his life could finally look like. In order to make that vision come true, Randy started studying the science of wealth and prosperity. He read hundreds of books and filled dozens of notebooks with the ideas that he learned. He went to seminars and workshops and started figuring out how to become not only successful but rich and prosperous. He adopted the motto, "I'll do today what others won't do, so in the future, I can do what others can't do," and he made it come true.

Today he lives in his dream home, packed with more designer clothes and shoes than an Armani boutique. He's in better health in his late forties than he was when he was twenty. He regularly travels around the world and schedules all of his business around playing on four different softball teams. He has a fleet of sports cars and luxury cars, and he wakes up to a view of sailboats on the bay. In the winter he's in Florida. In the summer you'll find him in Paris or Costa Rica. He travels the world right now, coaching others how to reach success.

* * *

These are great stories, aren't they? I love these stories. These are my friends. I love to surround myself with people like this, and that's what I've been able to do.

You'll be able to do that too when you make the decision to be rich and surround yourself with rich people. You might think that these are amazing people. They are not. They are regular folks, just like you, but you will notice they have some things in common. Each one of them started with nothing. Each one of them faced amazing adversity. Each of them had every excuse in the world to stay broke, yet all of them refused to do so. They all made the decision to be wealthy. They decided work harder, faster, smarter, and longer than anyone else. Every one of them studied success. They had goals, and they stuck with them even when it all sucked.

There are no extraordinary people. There are only regular people willing to do extraordinary things.

You can do extraordinary things. All you have to do is make the decision for your life to change and you can make that happen. Do you want to know how you can make it happen? Sure you do and I'm about to tell you.

So, here's where we are. Know where you are in terms of how much money you earn. Know where you are in terms of how much money you owe. Feel bad about your situation, and then get to work. That's what it's always going to come down to. You're saying, "Larry, but what should I do?"

Here's the good news. The next chapter is actually about what you have to do to move from where you are to a better place financially. I'm going to give you a plan. I'm going to give you tactics. I'm going to tell you exactly what you can do today in order to make a change in your financial picture.

5

How to Move to a Better Place Financially

've already told you that the most important thing for you to do is know where you are. You have to know how much money you have to work with. You have to know whom you owe to and how much you know. The next step would be to stop spending.

You've heard it. It's called the hole principle, which says when you find yourself in a hole, stop digging. In other words, stop spending money on anything you don't need. Stop spending money on anything except the necessities.

So, what are the necessities? Shelter. That would be your rent or your house payment, and that includes all of your utilities as well.

Then, food, and I mean eating conservatively at home. No going out. No fast food. No expensive restaurants. No restaurants of any type. Just the basic necessities of eating to get by.

Then pay your bills. You know what your bills are. Those are your obligations. That's money you've already spent that you owe someone, and you need to pay it back.

Those are the necessities. You're finished. You're done. You're cut off. That's where you spend your money.

Next I want you to keep a journal. Write down every single penny you spend. All of it, every single day. Categorize it according to shelter, clothes, utilities, insurance, and entertainment; even have a column for stupidity.

Yup, stupidity gets a column too, because sometimes you're going to spend some money on stupid things. You need to be able to recognize that, go back, and say, "That was a waste." Start writing down every single penny that you spend.

Then—you knew this was coming—as anybody who's ever written a book about prosperity says, cut up all your credit cards. Keep one—the kind that will work anyplace—for emergencies only.

I once worked with a woman who had over fifty credit cards. I told her she could keep one for an emergency. She decided to keep her Neiman Marcus card. Let me help you with this: shopping is not an emergency. To me, an emergency involves broken bones and blood, something that requires medical attention.

Don't get me wrong. I'm not against credit cards. There will be a point when you need them. I have several of them, but I pay them off. That's the rule. You have to be able to pay off the bill when it comes in, or at the very worst, you have to be able to pay it off next month. You have only sixty days to pay off everything on your credit card. That's all I'm giving you.

But don't cancel your credit cards. That can have a negative effect on your overall credit score. I'm just saying cut them up, so you can't carry them around and use them.

The Three Most Important Numbers in Your Life

Now I want to talk to you about the three most important numbers in your life. Know what they are.

If you're saying your IQ, you're wrong. The three most important numbers in your life are your credit score. Your credit score will determine whether you can get a loan and how much you're going to pay for that loan. It will have an impact on you forever. It's always going to be with you.

In fact, there are only two things you're never going to be without. One is your reputation, and the other is your credit rating. You can ruin both of these in an instant, and you may never be able to fix either one of them, because a bad credit score never goes away. You can take steps to fix it, and the bad ratings will eventually drop off, but if creditors dig deep enough—and some of them these days are digging very deep—those little credit dings are always going to show up. They'll be there like a dark cloud hovering over you.

So, you're in a bind. You have all this credit card debt. You have more bills than you have money. Here's what I want you to do: pick up the phone and contact all of the people you owe money to. Contact your creditors. Talk to them. Don't duck their phone calls. Don't hide from them. Don't ignore their letters. That's one of the biggest mistakes people make. Prove that you are willing to work with your creditors.

You see, I believe credit is judged on two things: the willingness to pay and the ability to pay. In the past, you haven't shown your willingness. It didn't matter whether you had the ability or not, but you haven't proved that you were willing to pay them, because you haven't paid them.

At this point I want you to turn that cycle around. Pick up the phone, contact your creditors, and tell them that you are now willing to pay them what you can. Explain that you don't have a high ability to pay them, but you do have the willingness.

Furthermore, don't pay someone to do this for you. There are lots of credit doctors out there who will happily contact your creditors for you simply because you're too embarrassed to do it. They're going to charge you for this service, and the more you hate doing it, the more they're probably going to charge you. You made this mess. Take responsibility for it and do it yourself.

Don't pay someone else to clean up a mess that you made. Get on the phone, talk to your creditors, explain your situation, and work out a payment plan that fits the amount of money you have right now. I promise you they would rather have a little bit of something than a whole lot of nothing.

In order to do this, you're going to have to set all your pride aside. Remember, they are not the guilty ones; you are. You need to show a little humility. Don't scream at them. They're doing their job, which is to collect their money. Remember, you used their money.

You have already proved to them that you can't be trusted. You have to change that, and the first way you change that is to show a little humility and prove to them that you are willing to work with them. So set your pride aside, get humble, and start talking and negotiating the best deal you possibly can.

This is not an easy process. It's going to be difficult. It's a hard thing to put yourself through, but it's something that you must do. You can't skip this integral part of getting out of debt. It will be discouraging, it will be humiliating, it will be embarrassing, but it's absolutely necessary. Remember, you made this mess. You have to get out of it.

Next I want you to get yourself a big calendar, one that you can stick on the wall or tape up on the refrigerator. I want it to have great big squares for each day of the month. On that calendar, write out all the bills that are due, the day they're due, and the day you need to send the payment in.

When you get to that date, and you send that payment in, get a big red pen and write "Paid" across that debt. Look at every single month and see that you're writing "Paid" in bright red. It will start to make you feel better about what you've been able to accomplish. It will also give you a picture of how you can start to budget according to how much money you're going to have and when you need to spend it.

Pay your bills as they come in. When a lot of people get a bill, they put it in a drawer or a basket, or they throw it over in the corner. Some people ignore those bills forever. Don't be one of those people. I want you to pay your bills the instant they come in. Sit down and write the check. Or go online and schedule it with your online banking. Regardless of how you do it, get it done and never fudge or convince yourself this is not an absolutely necessary part of your overall success because it is.

Here is a great little piece of advice that has always worked for me: make little payments on your bills. This is a trick I learned a long time ago. When a bill comes in—let's say it's for a credit card—make copies of the front page, the one that has your account number on it and lists the amount due. Make four or five copies of that page. Then get some envelopes and write out the address of the place where the payment needs to be sent. Use the main one to send in your main payment. That's the one that's the most important.

Throughout the month, as you start to see that you have a little bit of money—and I'm talking about a little bit; I don't care whether it's $5, $7, or $9—use that extra copy of the front page of your bill and mail in that $5 or $7 or $9 or whatever it is. You need to start making these little payments as often as you possibly can. The credit card companies won't like that, because it's a lot of extra work for them, but they will still accept your money, and you'll be eating away at your debt one tiny bite at a time.

If you bank online, this is a very easy thing to do online. I even do this right now myself. I go online and see whom I owe to. I say, "Wow, there's more than I thought I had there," so I'll start dumping the money on a daily basis, sometimes to pay off the few debts that I still have.

You can do this to pay off a car or make payments on your house. You can do it with any debt you owe by constantly making regular payments. Although they may seem small and insignificant, if you do it often enough, you will chip away at that debt. Before you know it, that debt will be gone.

Here's another little piece of advice: don't think you can borrow your way out of debt. It can't be done although you will be tempted. There are lots of stories right now about people who have borrowed against their equity. Now their house isn't worth what it once was, and they're upside down. They've borrowed against their equity, but their house isn't worth what they owe on it. Don't do that to pay off your bills. It's a ridiculous way to use your money. You're taking very temporary debt and turning it into long-term, permanent debt. Don't do that. You can't borrow your way out of debt. You have to pay your way out of debt, and you have to use the money you've earned.

See how it all works? You have to earn more money by working longer, harder, faster, and smarter. Then you have to use that money to pay off the debt that you've incurred.

It all comes back to the magic word *you*. Please don't ever think that you have the right to go to your family or your friends to borrow money. Don't mix family, friends, and finances. Just don't. You'll end up losing friends, and you'll cause resentment in your family forever. Stay away from that. Use the money you earned to pay off your debts.

Some people like to say, "I know how to get out of all this. I'll just declare bankruptcy." You've seen these television commercials with a smiling attorney who says, "If you have too many bills, and there isn't enough money to go around, bankruptcy is your answer."

That's an out-and-out lie. Bankruptcy is *an* answer, it might even be *the* answer, but it certainly shouldn't be your first answer. Don't think that you can bankrupt your way out of debt. You owe that money. Pay it off.

The number one reason people go bankrupt in America today is medical bills. Why do they have so many medical bills? This is a sad case. There could be lots of reasons. Of course, there are insurance issues, but you also need to be saving. You need to be putting money away. You need to have cash reserves to pay for anything that might come up.

Yet one of the main reasons people go broke is that they overspend. This just spend more money than they earn. It's dumb. Don't do it. That's why you have to have an excess of money. You have to be able to spend less on your necessities than you earn so you can have cash reserves, pay for insurance, and have an emergency fund in case something happens. You don't want to find yourself with a stack of medical bills that you can't pay and have to file bankruptcy to get out of them. And you certainly don't want to look at a bunch of useless crap and have to tell yourself that crap put you into bankruptcy. Do whatever it takes so you never find yourself in that situation.

Giving Up Things

You've done all the things that I've talked about, and you're still in trouble. What do you need to do next? Now it's about to get ugly. You need to start giving up some things.

The only way to get anything in life is to give up something else. So, if you want to get rich, if you want to get out of debt, what are you going to give up? You may have to give up golf. You may have to give up shopping or eating out. Those things make perfect sense, but you're going to have to give up some other stuff.

First of all, I want you to sell some things. Go through your house and look at what you're not using. If you didn't use something in the last thirty days, get rid of it. Go to the bad end of your closet. That's where you keep the clothes that you haven't worn in a good long while. They're out of style, they're out of date, and you're too fat to wear them anymore. Get those things out, take them to a resale store, and sell them.

Go through your house and take a hard look at the things that you can get rid of. You're probably going to get only about 10 cents on the dollar. I don't care; sell it anyway. You don't need it, it's just causing clutter, and it's a little bit of money that you can pay down on your debts.

Overall, debt can be a good thing, but credit card debt, the debt incurred from shopping and the other ridiculous things that we do with our money, is all bad debt. Debt that you have to pay 25 percent on—which is about what most people are paying on their credit cards right now—is bad debt. You have to get out of that debt, so start selling whatever you possibly can to pay down on your debts. Nothing is sacred.

Give up cable television. Oh, my goodness. Give up cable television? That's right. I don't care if you have to find some rabbit ears or roll up some aluminum foil and stick it on top of your set. You have to give up cable television. You don't need all those premium channels. I don't care if you're stuck with four major channels. I don't care how blurry it is. The point is, you can't afford it. You have to cut back wherever you can.

You might need to sell your car. The sad thing is you're probably upside down on your car. I don't care if you are upside down and you lose money in the process. If you need to get rid of your car because you can't afford the payment, that's something you need to do, and it can be done. It will be hard, but it can be done, which might mean that you have to get a much cheaper car in the process.

I don't care what you have to drive. That's not the point. The point is you have debts. You have an obligation to your family to provide them with financial security, and you can't do that as long as you're up to your ears in debt.

You might also have to move. You might have to find a cheaper place to live. I don't care how much trouble it's going to be. Just do it. It might mean you have to sell your house. It's a challenge, it's hard to sell your house, but you need to take whatever steps you possibly can. Meet with a licensed real estate agent. I'm not talking about somebody who can just sell houses. I'm talking about a real estate professional, someone who can actually consult with you about the right move for you to take with the real estate that you own.

Call your cell phone company to see if you can get a cheaper plan. Call your insurance agent and talk about how you can raise the deductible and lower your payment.

I want you to stop all eating out. Cut out going to the movies. You can't afford them right now. Give up your salon. Paint your own nails. Color your own hair. Give up the gym membership. You probably aren't using it anyway.

I worked with one guy who had four gym memberships, and he was still seventy-five pounds overweight. He hadn't been to the gym one time in a year, but he was still making payments on four different gym memberships. You know people like that; you may be one of those people. It doesn't make any sense to have that kind of gym membership. The number one excuse when I tell people that is, "But, Larry, I have a contract." I don't care. Go in and meet with the gym manager. Tell them that you don't have the money to pay them anymore and you're not going to. You want out of that contract. They will work with you.

I also want you to stop smoking. First of all, smoking is going to kill you, but mostly, you can't afford it. Do you realize that if you smoke just a one pack a day at $4 per pack, that's almost $1,500 a year? If you live for forty years (and it would be amazing if you did), that's almost $60,000. If you put that $1,500 a year in a tax-deferred savings account like an IRA or a 401(k) at 8 percent, do you realize that after forty years, you'd have $400,000? You could use that for retirement or your children's future or just to enjoy in your old age.

Are you willing to compromise not only your health and your life, but your financial future for a pack of cigarettes every single day? If you smoke more than a pack a day, just multiply that by how many packs you smoke. Stop smoking. Start saving the money.

Now you're probably saying, "Larry, this is all such a sacrifice." OK, fine. Don't do it. Really, I don't care. Stay broke. It's not up to me. I have money in the bank. I won't suffer one bit from what you do. You will. Your family will. Your future will suffer. But I won't. You're the one who has an issue, and if you have an issue that hurts you, you might want to be willing to change and be inconvenienced for a while.

I started this book by talking about being willing to do things differently. You have to prove that you're willing, and you have to take action. That's what I want you to do. I want you to prove that you're willing to make your life different. You do that by showing a willingness to change, and you do that by taking action.

If you don't want to do these things, that's fine, but if you want your life to be different, and I believe you do, you have to do some things differently. In order to have what you never had and get something you have never gotten; you have to do something you've never done, which means you're going to have to change the way you live. You have to change the way you live in order to get new results.

Probably not one thing I've said to you so far has been a surprise. You've heard these things before. There are lots of guys on television talking about them. You pick up any book on how to get rich or how to get out of debt, and they're going to say exactly what I've just said.

Small Things

Now I want to give you a couple of things that a lot of people don't say and maybe you hadn't thought of before. Again, these are small things, but remember you got into debt. You got into financial trouble with little bitty things. Those are the things that always bite us in the butt. Let me give you some small things that can help you get out of trouble.

One option I find interesting today is checking accounts that will round up the amount of the check you write and put the odd cents into a savings account. For instance, if you write a check for

$19.63, they're going to take $20 out of your account. They'll take the 37-cent difference and put it into a savings account, so it can start building interest. I promise you will never miss those 37 cents, yet over a period of time, it will be amazing how that will build up.

Let me give you another idea. Pick up all the change you see on the streets; pick up every penny. I am amazed at how many people see a penny on the street and walk right over it saying, "It's just a penny." Do you realize that a penny is interest on $1 for one month? Pick it up and put it in your pocket. I have jars in my closet full of change that I've picked up.

The other thing you can do is start saving all the change that you have at the end of the day. You may say, "I do that all the time." Good. Keep doing it. In fact, break a dollar whenever you can so you'll have the change. You'll be amazed at the end of the year: hundreds of dollars will have built up.

Some people say, "Larry, it's ridiculous to constantly bend over picking up change and breaking dollars to have change." Change builds up. Don't discount this idea. In fact, every single morning for years and years, I get up saying, "Money comes to me from all directions," and it does. One direction it comes from is the pavement. It's down there. Bend over and pick it up.

I know that penny won't make you rich, but it will give you more money than you had before you picked it up. You see, if your goal is to always have more money, somehow that's more money. I'm not getting all New Agey on you. I'm just telling you to develop a consciousness that you're looking for different ways to have more money in life. That's more money.

When I was a little boy, my dad used to play a game with me; it was about pennies. He said, "Son, if I hired you to go to work for me, and I agreed to pay you one penny on your very first day, but I would double your salary every single day that you work for me, so the second day you'd make two pennies, and the next day you'd make four pennies, and the next day after that, you'd make eight pennies, would you take the job?"

I'd say, "No. No way I'm going to work for just a penny, because at the end of the week, it's just a few more pennies. Dad, that doesn't even make sense."

He told me to get a sheet of paper and figure it out. It's really cool. In fact, you can do this with your kids, and they will be amazed. I got out a sheet of paper, and I started to figure it out I started out on day one with one penny, day two with two pennies.

By the time I got to the end of the week, day seven, I had sixty-four pennies. What's amazing is that by the time you get to day thirty doing this, you're making $5,368,000 on that one day. Is that cool? If somebody ever comes up to you and says, "I want to offer you a job today for a penny, and tomorrow I'll double it" and so on, take it. I bet they're not going to do it, but it's still a cool way to start thinking about small amounts of money and the impact they can have on your life.

Here's the next thing I want you to do: carry cash. I'm a big believer in carrying cash. Here's why: when it's gone, it's gone. When you're out of cash, you're done. With a credit card, you slide right past zero—even with a debit card. People argue with me: "Yeah, but, Larry, I have a debit card. That's the same thing." Bull. It's not the same thing. Don't trick yourself into thinking that way.

Don't believe the commercials on television that show the lines screeching to a halt because a guy reaches in his pocket and pulls out a handful of cash to pay for his latte. You need to carry cash. Put the credit cards away; cut them up. You've already done that, but also do it with your debit card, because you can slide right past zero with a debit card too. Carry cash.

If you have $200 to buy groceries for the month, get an envelope, write "Groceries" on the outside, and stick $200 in it. When you go to the grocery store, reach into that envelope, and buy your groceries out of it. When the envelope is empty, you're done buying groceries.

This may seem like a ridiculous process to you, and you may think, "I'm smarter than this. I don't have to do it." No, you're not. That's why you're in a bind. That's why you have debt. You haven't been able to control your spending. This is just one little thing you can do to control it. Do this in every single area where you can pay cash—things like groceries and going to the gas station. You can do this.

Here's one that's going to amaze you. Stop buying food in bulk. I love those big warehouse stores. I love to go up and down those aisles, and I am amazed at the bargains you can get there. Really, you can get some great deals, but ask yourself, "Do I really need a four-pack of sixty-four-ounce bottles of ketchup?" Chances are you don't.

I don't care how much of a bargain it is per ounce. You don't need it, so don't buy it. The only things you want to buy in bulk are those that you're going to constantly use up, like toilet paper, paper towels, and tissues. That's what you need to buy in bulk, not food. Stop buying food in bulk. It doesn't make any sense. It ends up actually costing you more in the long run.

I've gone into those warehouse stores to buy one little thing and walked out with a basket that cost me $200. I'll bet you've done the same thing. Be careful buying in bulk.

Next, I want you to change your language. Stop talking and thinking as if you're broke. Stop saying, "I can't afford . . ." Those three little words will make you think of yourself as a victim. Stop thinking that you can't afford it. Get in control of your money.

Instead start saying things like, "I don't choose to spend the money I have right now on that item." That puts you in control. You don't choose to spend the money. That's much different than "I can't afford that" or "That costs too much."

You have to start getting in control and stop thinking like a victim. You are in charge of how much money you have. You are in charge of how quickly you get out of debt. You are in control of your future—no one else. How much things cost has no relevance to how much money you have. You're in control.

Here's one that's going to bother a lot of people. If you want to have more money, lose weight and clean up your house. Now you're saying, "What in the world does that have to do with money?" It has everything to do with money.

If your spending is out of control, there's a very good chance that other parts of your life are out of control too. Let me give you a couple of observations. I know these are broad, sweeping generalizations, and there are exceptions, but I've found them to be true in almost all cases.

People who are out of control with their spending are usually out of control with their eating. In other words, people who spend big usually eat big. People who are out of control with their spending are usually out of control in their relationships. People who have relationship problems normally have money problems. People who are out of control with their spending are also usually out of control when it comes to keeping their houses and cars clean. Lack of discipline in any area shows up in other areas.

Here's a challenge. Go to any of the television channels that talk about how to clean up your house and organize your life. Watch the shows about the people whose lives are full of chaos. Their bedrooms are stacked waist-deep with stuff they don't need. I'll guarantee you that the people in those shows are overweight. I'll guarantee you that they have money problems.

I have done a television show about people with money problems and I've noticed that many of the people who have money problems also live in houses that are full of chaos. I notice that they have relationship problems. Their houses are dirty, their cars are dirty, they have problems at work.

If you have a problem in any area of your life, it is probably running into other areas too. Get control of your life. When you get control of one area, chances are you'll get control of other areas, so go on a diet. Go on a physical diet. Go on a financial diet. Go through your house and clean it up. Start getting rid of things you don't need.

The more order you put into your life in one area, the more order you will start to put into every other area of your life. This is not a complicated thing.

As long as we're talking about weighing a little less, I want you to eat a little less. Now you're saying again, "What difference does it make, Larry?" You're spending too much on groceries. The average American spends way too much on groceries. The average American right now spends $2,500 a year eating out. If you're in a family of four, that's $10,000 a year you spend eating out. You have to cut back on that.

I worked with one couple who spent $20,000 a year eating out, and they still spent $18,000 a year on groceries: $38,000 for two people to eat every single year. That was more than one of them even earned per year on their salary. It's no wonder they were both overweight. One way to fix their money problem was to spend less on their food.

First of all, cut out all eating out. We've already talked about this. Second, when you go to the grocery store, don't buy prepared meals. I mean, really, come on. You don't have to have somebody else cook your chicken or mash your potatoes for you. It's not that hard. I'm not asking you to be Betty Crocker here. I'm just asking you to fix some basic meals.

I've also noticed this: healthy foods cost less. Fresh vegetables cost less. Spend your money buying things like meat, chicken, fish, vegetables, and whole-grain breads and cereal. Buy lots of fruit. If you spend less on your food, it will be the right thing to do from a health standpoint; it'll be also the right thing for you to do for your food budget.

Here's what I suggest: $75 per person per week. That's a great plan. With two people in the family, you get $150 a week to eat on. That's maximum. Chances are you spend that much eating crap and having a drink all by yourself on just one meal.

That's great IF you can afford it. If you can't, follow my plan. Anybody can eat very well using that as a financial plan for how much money to spend at the grocery store. Just make the decision, shop smart, and start buying things that are healthy for you.

Take a Tough Look at Your Friends

Here's one that you don't hear very often: take a tough look at your friends. I've already mentioned that Jim Rohn is one of my very favorite speakers, trainers, consultants, and authors. I learned more from him over the years than from probably any other single person, and he said that your income will be an average of those of your five closest friends. I believe that to be true.

Here's a little exercise for you. Write down the names of your five closest friends and write down roughly how much money they make. (Don't pick up the phone and call them. You know about how much money they make.) Add it all up, divide by five, and I'll bet that's pretty close to how much money you make.

What does that mean? If you want to have more money, you have to dump your friends and get smarter, richer friends. Yup, that's going to be tough. What's important to you? Being able to provide a financially secure future for your family or having a bunch of loser friends who aren't moving you closer to where you want to be?

What do your friends talk about? Do they make fun of other people, especially rich people? Do they just sit around putting other people down? Do they gripe and whine all the time about work and how unfair life is?

Ask yourself this: What do your friends expect from you? Do they expect the best from you or are they the kind of people that come up, put their arm around you, and say, "It's a cold, cruel world out there. It's okay that you're broke, lazy and make bad decisions" because chances are they're broke, lazy and make bad decisions too.

That's not the kind of friend you want. It's not a cold, cruel world. A true friend is somebody who's going to come up to you and say, "What are you thinking? What was on your mind when you did that? Are you crazy? Stop doing that."

A friend will kick your butt. A friend will expect the best from you. A friend will be absolutely intolerant of anything but the best when it comes to you. That's what a real friend is.

A friend is not a person who's going to drag you down. A friend is a person who's going to lift you up and make you stand there on your own two feet. That's the kind of friend you want.

What do your friends let you get by with? If they're letting you get by with too much, you might want to decide if they're really friends or not.

Here's a big one: what kind of books do your friends have you reading? If you say, "Books?" that might be a clue. That might not be the kind of friend you want. Friends ought to be suggesting better ways for you to live your life, because they're trying to figure out ways to live their own lives better.

So, take a look at your friends. How much money do they have? Decide whether that's the kind of friend you really want to have or not. I know this is a cold, hard look at people, but you know what? You become like the people you hang around. Hang around better people, and you will become a better person.

The Science of Charity

Here's a big one, and you might think it's contradictory to everything I've said so far. I want you to give away some money. I know, I know. Here I've told you to stop spending money on anything except the necessities. I told you to focus on your debt, save all you can, have an emergency fund, and now I'm telling you to just go out there and give it away. It doesn't even make sense, does it? You're right, it doesn't make any sense, but it works.

When you're willing to share part of what you've earned with other people, somehow—I don't know how—it magically comes back to you. I don't know why it works. I just know that it works.

In fact, here's a quick story about that. After my business failure and my personal bankruptcy, I was broke. I mean, I was really broke. I was so broke that I couldn't pay attention. I was so broke, my cash bounced. I didn't have any money. I couldn't afford to pay my bills. I certainly couldn't afford to give any money away. I was barely making it.

Yet I had been raised with the idea that you should always share part of what you have. No matter how little you have, you should share it with other people.

I was sitting at my desk, and I got an overwhelming urge, which I could not explain, to give some money away. The problem was I didn't have much money to give away. As I said, I was in a bind.

I pulled out my checkbook, and I saw that I had $100. It was really all the money I had, and I had two little boys, and Christmas coming up, and bills that needed to be paid, but I couldn't help it; I knew

I had to do something charitable. So, I wrote out a check to my favorite charity. I put it in an envelope, and I left my office immediately to go the post office and put it in the mail. I was afraid that if I held on to it too long, I would back out and wouldn't put the check in the mail.

I dropped the check in the mail, and it was done. I felt great, but I was also a little afraid to go home and tell my wife that I'd just spent $100 we really couldn't afford to spend, by giving it away.

That evening I was sitting at home, trying to figure out how to tell my wife that I'd just given away $100, when my doorbell rang. It was my attorney. Since most attorneys don't make house calls, I didn't think this was going to be good news, but I did invite him in. He told me that someone had just called him to forgive him of a huge debt that he owed in his business, and he wanted to pass along his good fortune by forgiving some of his debtors.

Then the attorney handed me the statement on my account; it had been forgiven. He told me to have a nice evening, and he walked out. I looked down at that statement, and I realized that I owed him $100. That $100 had just been forgiven.

Some might say, "Boy, that's an interesting coincidence, Larry." Yeah, maybe, but for me, it was a lesson. It was a lesson that no matter how hard it gets you can always afford to give something away. There's always a way you can give something.

I don't quote preachers very often, and I don't care what you think of them, but I grew up around Tulsa, Oklahoma, so Oral Roberts was everywhere. I heard him say something that I've never forgotten: "A rejected opportunity to give is a lost opportunity to receive." You need to memorize that. Even though things might be tough for you, you need to figure out a way to give away at least a small amount of money. When you prove that you're willing to give some money away, I think you open up channels for receiving it.

That's what I'm looking for. I'm looking for you to open up the channels, because money flows. Money comes to you as it goes from you. If you are unwilling to give any money away, you prove that you lack trust that money's ever going to come back to you.

If your hand is gripped so tight that you can't release what you have, you won't be able to open up your hand in order to receive more. Is this philosophical? Spiritual? I guess maybe it is. It doesn't matter what it is. The point is that it works.

To help you with this, I want you to make another list. Sit down right now and write a list of everything that you're thankful for in your life. Now you may be saying, "Larry, I don't have very much, so what do I have to be thankful for?"

You could have a whole lot less so sit down right now and write down what you do have. You have a lot to be thankful for. The fact that you were able to read this book is something to be thankful for. Again, reduce it to the ridiculous, but remember, you must be thankful for what you have.

Zig Ziglar, one of the greatest motivational speakers of all time, said, "The more you are thankful for what you have, the more you will have to be thankful for." That's another line that I committed to memory. You need to remember that and practice it in your life.

Take a minute to write down everything in your life that you're thankful for. That will help you to be more charitable.

I Can't Help Them

I get dozens of emails every single month from people who are concerned about family members who are in financial trouble. Some of those letters are very sad. They are desperate cries for help. They are clearly written out of both love for that family member and the pain caused by watching that person suffer. These people want me to help them to help their family members with their money issues. They've already tried everything they know to do and they're absolutely at their wit's end about what they can say and do to help that family member wake up and turn things around.

Sadly, I have to tell them that I can't help them, and I can't help their family member that's in trouble either. If somebody doesn't want to be helped then they can't be helped. People change when they want to change, not when you want them to change. They change when there's no better option for them and not when they need to change. They change when they have to change because the pain of not changing is so great they finally have no other choice.

Sometimes you have to let people hit rock bottom. You have to stop enabling people. You have to stop helping them. I know that's sad but it's just a bit of tough love. I've discovered that no good comes from helping people suffer in comfort. And nothing but frustration comes from helping people who need help. You have to help people who want it and want it so badly they will do whatever it takes.

So, allow people to become uncomfortable. Allow them to hurt just a little, especially when it's your kids. I know that's a hard thing to do. When we see our kids are in trouble, the natural thing to do is to want to step in and save them. Be we do them a disservice when we do that. Kids have to learn from their own mistakes. You can't constantly be there to bail them out, especially when it comes to money. Besides, kids learn everything they know about money from their parents. And if your kids are having money problems, chances are, you didn't teach them very good lessons.

Money and Your Kids

Teach your kids what they need to know about money. Teach them what a mortgage is. Show them that although a house may cost $300,000, it really costs much more when you spread it out over twenty or thirty years. Show them what that house really costs with interest. Talk to them about utility bills. Talk to them about how the more you leave the lights on and the doors open, the more the utility bill goes up.

Kids don't understand that stuff. You have to explain to them how money works, what interest is and how easy it is to get in trouble with credit cards. Teach them that a deal is a deal. Teach them that when you make a deal with a credit card company or to buy a car or with a utility company or mortgage company, that it's not only a contract to pay but a moral and ethical obligation. Teach them that when you've given your word you have to live up to it. You have to pay your bills when you said you would.

Show them what you're doing personally to deal with your own debt. Talk to them about the mistakes you've made and the steps you are making to correct them. Sadly, we all want our kids to have it better than we had. I say that's sad, because when we think that way, even though it's normal, we indulge our children way too much.

I've gone into the clothes closets of people who have one-year-olds. They have hundreds of outfits for a one-year-old baby, clothes with tags still on them that that baby is never going to be able to wear. They're going to outgrow them way too fast to ever even spit up on them. The child would have had more fun if you'd just given them the cardboard box that the clothes came in.

Your obligation as a parent is to teach your kids to be responsible with their money, not to indulge them with your money. You need to teach them how to earn their own money. Give them chores so they can earn money. Encourage them to do things around the neighborhood to earn money. Then teach your kids how to save a little bit of money, how to share a little bit of it, and how to enjoy some of it. I'm big on enjoying money. There certainly should be a point in your life where you have enough extra money that you can set some of it aside to enjoy. The problem is that most of us enjoy it way too much and don't meet our obligations. Teach your kids how to separate their money into different piles: some to share, some to save, some to enjoy, and some to pay your obligations. That is your responsibility. It's your job. And if you don't do it, it's a dereliction of duty.

At some point in your life, when your kids are older and get in financial trouble (and they will), you will need to make some tough decisions. You will need to decide whether you're going to bail them out or lend them the money.

Here's the problem. Lending money to family members makes you a collection agency. Is that a position you want to be in with your kids? Do you want put yourself in the position of having to say, "Listen, this is the amount of money I lent you. This is when you said you'd pay me back, and you haven't done it."?

Believe me, they're going to play the guilt card. They're going to say, "I'm your baby. Is that how you want to treat me? Don't you love me?" Then it goes South. They will get mad. And that will make you mad. The relationship will be damaged, maybe forever, all over some money.

When your kids get in trouble and you start to bail them out, decide up front whether it's going to be a loan or a gift. I think you should bail them out when they've really learned their lesson.

Along those lines, let me talk about cosigning. You're going to be prone to cosign for your kids. It seems somehow like your parental duty. Sometimes it works out but often it doesn't, and you aren't aware they are falling behind on their payments. You think all you're doing is signing your name in order to help them get some credit to buy something they need or want. What you're really doing is agreeing to pay that debt off in case they don't.

Don't cosign for anyone at any time, in any situation, even for your kids. It rarely has a happy ending.

Here's another controversial idea when it comes to kids and money: Your kids are not entitled to your money when you die. Now I know that bothers a bunch of folks. Some people say it is important to leave your kids something. I agree that it is important to leave your kids something. You just don't need to leave them any money.

I have no intention of leaving my kids any money. On the last day I'm alive, if I know when that is, I plan on spending all the money I have. I don't owe my kids the money I worked hard to earn. Now you're probably saying, "That's selfish." Maybe, but you know what I owe my kids? I owe my kids the knowledge of how to earn, save, invest and enjoy their money. That's what you owe your kids too. If you do that, you're a good parent.

Your New Budget

It's time to talk about your new budget. This is your goal: Live on less than you earn. Period, with no excuses.

I don't want to hear your excuses. No one else does either. The last people who want to hear your excuses are your creditors. We're just dealing with numbers here. Numbers don't have emotions. They don't lie and they don't have any feelings or care about what you want or what you think you need. A budget is a document with numbers that reflect your financial status and a guide to control your spending. So, get a sheet of paper and get started.

Begin your budgeting process with the end in mind. First of all, write down your monthly income.

That's all the money you have to work with, no more. It has to cover all of your expenses – every dime you spend on anything. Write down how much money you make on a monthly basis after taxes.

Then write down things like your mortgage or your rent, your monthly car payment, personal loans, and credit cards, as well as other monthly expenses like insurance, utilities, internet, water, telephone, cell phone, gasoline, groceries, dry cleaning—every single thing that you're obligated to pay.

By this point, you were already supposed to have cut back on things like your gym membership, entertainment, and eating out. If you have any of those things left in your budget, you have to write them down.

Decide how much money you're going to put into savings and how much you're going to give away. Ten percent for savings and ten percent for charity is a good place to start. Now, take how much you have to spend and subtract it from how much you earn. Hopefully, that will be a positive number. If not, go back to all of your expenses and start cutting them back anywhere you can. Except for the savings and charity. Don't cut those.

You're probably saying, "Larry, this is tough. This is ugly. How do I make it all fit?"

I don't care how you make it fit. It's not up to me; it's up to you. You can't survive by spending more money than you earn. Do what it takes to make it fit. Keep slashing your expenses until you figure it out or until you figure out a way to earn more money. Maybe you ought to get another job, or two more jobs.

You're going to have to do something to get to the position where you spend less than you earn. When you're in that position, you have a shot at getting ahead but not until then.

Your aim is to have excess money left over after this budgeting process. That excess is what will allow you to become more financially secure through investments.

How to Invest And Enjoy

How do you invest? There are lots of ways to do it. First of all, hire a professional to help you. That's what I do. I'm good at earning money; I'm not all that great at investing it. I don't have the time to become great at investing money. The best I could ever become would be an amateur investor. I want an amateur handling my money. I want to hire somebody who makes more money than I do. I want to hire a rich, successful person who makes their living and got rich through their investing their own money and who has a track record of helping other people get rich investing. That's the person I want to trust with my money.

Lastly, remember that money's main purpose is freedom and enjoyment. You want the freedom to do whatever you want to do, when you want to do it, the way you want to do it and with whom you want to do it. That freedom is all money really gives you. That's what makes it enjoyable.

I want you to be able to go to the best restaurants you can possibly afford. I want you to dress any way you want to dress. I want you to wear great watches and amazing jewelry, drive wonderful cars, take amazing vacations. I want you to give huge amounts to charity. I want you to get a massage or facial whenever you want one. It makes no sense to bust your butt getting rich and then live as if you're barely getting by. The problem is we live as if we're rich when we're barely getting by.

I want you to reverse that. I want you to tighten your belt right now until you have excess money so you can invest it and ultimately have all the freedom and the wonderful things that money brings you.

Can you do it? You can. The question is never whether you can. The question is always whether you will. You have to be willing to do what it takes to get what you want. You're able. You can. But are you willing? You're going to find out pretty quick.

I've never said it was easy. It isn't. It's hard. It's really tough to go from getting by or being broke to getting ahead and getting rich. I know it's hard. I've done it so I know how hard it is. You're not telling me anything new. But I'm telling you right now, you can do it.

You might not become a millionaire. You might barely become a thousandaire. But when you make the decision to do it you can get farther ahead than where you are. It can be done. It is possible.

I grew up on a chicken farm in Muskogee, Oklahoma. It was called Henry's Bantam Ranch. My Dad raised bantam chickens. We also had lots of rabbits, goats, pigs, a horse, a donkey and a couple of cows.

One day when I was a little boy, we had a new calf born. I was there with my dad when the calf was being born. It was so small and cute that I immediately picked it up and hugged on it. My Dad said, "Son, if you pick up that calf today, and you pick it up tomorrow, and you pick up that calf every single day of its life and you never miss a day, you'll be able to pick up that calf when it's full-grown."

I was skeptical. He explained to me that the calf would grow a little bit every day, but it wouldn't grow so much that I couldn't pick it up every single day, as long as I never missed a day. He said, "Larry, if you ever miss a day, you're not going to be able to do it." It still didn't seem possible to me. I was standing there looking at this calf's mother, and that cow probably weighed 300 pounds. I could not imagine picking up a 300-pound cow, but I trusted my dad.

I told my dad I'd do it. Right then, I reached over, picked up that calf again, and said to myself, "That's day one." The next day, I went out to the barn again, grabbed the calf, picked it up, and said to myself, "No problem. Day two." The next day I did the same thing. Every single day that week, I walked out to the barn, picked up that calf, and thought, "This is going to be a breeze. I can do it."

Then it rained. I got busy. I had to play with my friends and all that stuff, so I missed a day. The next day I went out to the barn and realized it was a little harder to pick up the calf. My Dad just laughed and said, "I told you, you can't miss a day. If you want to do what seems impossible, you can never miss a day."

Then it got busy again, and I missed a couple of days. When I went out to the barn the next time with my Dad, I couldn't pick the calf up. No matter how hard I tried, I couldn't. My Dad laughed and said again, "Larry, if you want to do what seems impossible, you can never miss a day."

I'm not sure I'd ever have been able to pick up a 300-pound cow. Actually, I doubt it and think my Dad might have been messing with me. After all, a 300-pound cow is a little hard to get your arms around. But I never forgot the lesson. If you want to achieve what seems to you to be impossible, you can never miss a day of working on it. It's the daily discipline and the daily work that makes achieving things possible.

The impossible doesn't care whether you're busy. The impossible doesn't care when it's raining or when you don't feel good or when you want to go play with your friends. The impossible requires that you do what you have to do every single day.

At this point, maybe getting rich seems impossible to you. Maybe even getting back to even seems impossible to you. I remember very well when it did for me. The whole concept probably feels like something you just can't get your arms around, but you know what? It doesn't matter. You still have to do a little bit toward getting rich every single day. You have to spend a little less. You have to save a little more. You have to pay a little bit more on your debts. You have to read a little more. You have to think a little harder, work a little harder, work a little longer, and work a little faster. You have to do it all every single day, and you can never miss a day.

6

Your Life and Your Beliefs

'
've spent a lot of time explaining how to run a better business, work harder, and work smarter. I've talked to you about your money. I've explained to you how to spend money, get out of debt, move beyond where you are to a better place, possibly even become a millionaire.

Now it's time to wrap it up and talk about all areas of your life. I want to talk about you and what you believe. Your beliefs determine everything in your life. What you believe about money determines how much money you have. What you believe about women determines how you're going to treat your wife and daughter. What women believe about men determines how they treat their husband and sons. These things determine how you treat your boss and coworkers and customers. What you believe about yourself determines how you dress, whether your clothes are clean and fashionable, and whether you shine your shoes or not. What you believe about love determines how much of it you give; how much you receive and how much of it you're experiencing in every area of your life. What you believe about success determines how much success you have. What you believe about happiness determines if you're happy or not.

See how it works? What you believe to be true in your life is what you experience in your life.

If you believe you're a loser, you're going to live the life of a loser. If you believe that you can achieve great things, you increase your chances of achieving great things. I'm not going to be one of those typical motivational guys who says that as long as you believe it, you can achieve it. That is not what I'm telling you here at all. I don't believe most of that mumbo-jumbo motivational stuff. However, I know that your chances of being successful in all areas of life and business increase based on what you believe to be true about yourself. Why? Because you always act on your beliefs and rarely act contrary to your beliefs. That's the key. It's the action that come about as a result of your beliefs.

What are your beliefs? Do you believe that the world is a bad place and that opportunities are hard to come by? Then you're going to have a hard time getting by. If you believe that you live in a land where opportunities are endless, and you can create a life of wealth, health, prosperity, success, and happiness, that's what you're going to experience.

Work with me on this. Take a sheet of paper and write down what you believe to be true about yourself and about life. At the end, I'm going to prove to you that that's exactly the kind of life you're living. So, yes, again, indulge me and take a few minutes to write down what you believe to be true about your life and yourself.

You've done it, right? You've written down the things that you believe about yourself and about life. I'll guarantee you that's the kind of life you're living. If you want to change the kind of life you're living, you have to change what you think. You have to change what you say and what you do. What you think about, talk about, and do something about is what comes about in your life.

So, to be really clear: To change your results, change everything that creates those results. Change your thinking, beliefs, words and actions.

Look at your results. Your results are a reflection of what you believe. Results are a reflection of how you think. Results tell me how you talk about yourself and others. Results tell me what you do every single day. You want new results? Then change those things. It's that simple. Do you remember what you did yesterday? If you don't like the results you got yesterday, change the actions you took.

If somebody told me all I had to do to be more successful was change the way I brush my teeth, I'd brush my teeth differently. I'd use a different hand. I'd get a new toothbrush or a different tube of toothpaste. I would do whatever it took to change my results if I didn't like my results. I'd get out on the other side of the bed. I'd drive to work by a different direction. I'm would be willing anything. Regardless of what you're doing, figure out how you can do it differently, how you can do it better, how you can do it smarter, how you can do it faster. Then do it and watch your results change.

Design a Different Life

In order to have a different life, you actually have to design a different life. Most people spend more time planning their day off than they do planning their lives. I want you to take a minute and decide what you want your life to look like.

What would you like to accomplish before you die? What do you want to own that you don't currently own? Before, I was explaining how to budget and how to design a life from a financial standpoint, but now I want you to scope up. Think much more about what kind of relationship you'd like to have with your spouse, your family, and your coworkers.

What would you like to be able to do, and where would you like to be able to go? Scope up much more than we talked about when we were just talking about money. Design the kind of life you want to live, and then move to the next section, which is this: what are you doing to make it happen?

This is where it's going to get tough. What are you actually doing? What actions are you taking to make that life come about? Chances are, not very much. I'm sorry, but that's the truth. Chances are, you're not doing very much to make the kind of life you want to live happen. Chances are, you're just kind of trudging along with the way things are. You get up, and you do today what you did yesterday.

That's the problem. Doing what you did yesterday is only going to get you the same things that you got yesterday. If that's not what you want your life to look like, you have to do things differently.

Write down right now what you're doing. Short list? Probably. Now decide what you could be doing. You know what you could be doing? A whole lot more than you're doing right now.

Could you be reading more? Could you be studying more? Could you be taking an extra class at night? Could you be working an extra job? Could you be spending more time with your family? Of course. You could do more than you are right now. The purpose of this exercise is to get you thinking in a way that will allow you to act differently so you can achieve more and have better results.

I'm not one of those typical motivational guys who allows you to just sit back and believe that as long as you have a good attitude and expect the best from your life, everything is going to be fine.

I've had a good, positive attitude all my life, and I've had plenty of crap happen to me. Having a good, positive attitude doesn't keep anything from happening to you. It just allows you to deal with the crap that does happen to you. That's what you need—the ability to deal with what happens to you. Why? Because it's going to happen to you. That's how life really is. You need the ability to deal with what happens to you and that takes attitude, skill, planning, knowledge and everything else you can add to your arsenal.

The Power of Negative Thinking

I'm a big proponent of having a negative attitude. Now you're saying, "What? Who would possibly encourage me to have a negative attitude?" Me.

In order to make a positive change in your life you first have to get negative about your life. You need to say, "I'm better than this. I deserve better than this. I want more than I have right now." You need to be your own best friend by kicking your own butt and refusing to tolerate anything except the best from yourself. That's how you get ahead.

You can't sit around with rose-colored glasses on and a big ol' happy face and pretend that it's all going to be okay. Chances are that it's not going to be okay. Certainly not unless you take responsibility, take control and get to work.

I'm telling you right now that you can have more than you've ever had before and you can become more than you've ever been before, but it's going to take hard work. It's going to take recognizing what your talents are and it's going to take using those talents to achieve more in order to produce better results. That takes a whole lot more than just a positive attitude. It takes getting negative about your situation so you will recognize the need to do more.

The Advantages of Discomfort

You sometimes hear the folks who say, "As long as I feel really good about myself, I can go out there and accomplish anything." I can assure you that you've never made one positive change in your whole life from feeling good about yourself. We don't make positive change in our lives when we feel good about who we are. I've already explained this to you. We make positive change in our lives when we become uncomfortable with who we are. That's how it really works.

Your goal should be to go out and create discomfort in your life. Don't rely on me to make you uncomfortable. Hopefully, I've made you uncomfortable enough to be willing to take action, but you're not always going to be reading this book. You need to create your own discomfort. Remind yourself that when you're becoming just a little bit too comfortable, that's when you need to make a change. And you don't really want to wait for life to make your uncomfortable. If your finances make you uncomfortable, you're already in trouble. If your relationships are becoming uncomfortable, you should have been doing something different long ago. If you're unhealthy, that's a sign that you haven't been taking care of yourself. Life signaling you that you aren't doing well means that you got lazy and weren't paying attention and that you were comfortably falling apart. That's why you need to get ahead of it all and create your own discomfort in advance when you can.

Let me give you an example about what motivation really is to me and when you realize you have to make a change. I read a survey recently that said at least 68 percent of our society right now is twenty-five pounds overweight. If you don't believe that, look down. If it doesn't apply to you, just look around. You will find out that what I'm saying is true.

We have a lot of heavy folks out there. Typically, as you start to gain weight, you buy bigger clothes and you start to wear a lot of black. Look around. When you see folks wearing a lot of black, it's probably not because they are being stylish, it's probably because they're trying to cover up an extra twenty.

So, you buy bigger clothes, and you buy them in black, until you get to the point where you can stand in front of the mirror and say, "You know, I still look pretty good." As long as you can look in the mirror and say, "I still look pretty good," you're never going to lose a pound. You're not going to do one damn thing about it because you have convinced yourself that you look okay. You don't do anything about it until it's 3:00 in the morning and you have to get out of bed to go to the bathroom. You flip on the bathroom light and catch a glimpse of yourself in the mirror, naked, and you say, "Damn. I'm huge." That's motivation. So, strip yourself down (metaphorically please) and go to the mirror of life and say, "I deserve better. I'm a mess. I know it. I see it. I'm going to fix it."

Motivational Myths

There are a lot of motivational myths. You've heard them all before, I'm sure. You've heard that you can do whatever you want to do. No, you actually can't do whatever you want to do. You can do more than you think you can do but you can't just to whatever you want to do. Believing that is only going to lead to huge disappointments. You can do whatever you have the talent to do and you have the talent to do a whole lot more than you're doing right now. You haven't been willing to apply the talents that you have and work hard using them. When people say you can have whatever you want to have, that is not true either. You can have what you are willing to work hard enough to earn. That's what you can have. If you aren't willing to earn it, then you don't get to have it.

There are no problems, only opportunities. The motivational bozos love to tell you that. What planet are these people from? I have problems. You have problems. We all have problems. They are not opportunities. They're problems, and they have to be dealt with like problems.

I like to look at things as they really are. A problem is a problem. Hurt is real. Pain exists. Learn how to deal with it. It doesn't do you any good to sugarcoat your situation.

Then you have those bozos who say, "Just go out there and give it 110 percent." Oh yeah, that's the key to success. Go out there and give it 110 percent. In fact, I'll bet you've said that before. There are even people out there wearing little lapel pins that say, "110 percent." Here's the problem: You can't give it 110 percent. It's impossible. 100 percent is all there is. And all there is, is all there is. That's pretty much why they call it all there is. Chances are, you aren't doing all there is. Chances are, you're giving a whole lot less than 100 percent, but I'll guarantee you, you can't give 110 percent.

It's like being on the airplane and hearing the flight attendant say, "Today's flight will be extremely full." No, it won't. It can't be *extremely* full. It can only be full. Full is all there is. If it's extremely full, you probably have somebody riding on the wing or something.

This one's become very popular because this is one of those circle-up, hold hands, and sing "Kumbaya" lines: The key to all success, happiness and prosperity is to just be yourself. Yeah, right. That'll work. Just be yourself. What if you're stupid? What if you're a jerk? What if you're a stupid jerk? Why don't you be somebody else. Please.

Then they'll tell you, "But, Larry, you're perfect just the way you are." Chances are, that's a lie too. You're not perfect just the way you are. Don't believe that for a minute. Spiritually you may be perfect just the way you are. And while God may love and accept you just the way you are, the rest of us don't like you. You might need to change who you are a bit so the rest of us can tolerate you.

You have to be careful about what the motivational bozos are saying. Too many are claiming that they're changing people's lives or that they're changing the world. The world doesn't change. People don't want to change either. The world will change when it wants to or when it gets so bad there is no other choice. Same for people. Reading a self-help book won't change your life. Going to an event won't change your life either. Or your business. Those things provide the information you can use to make the change but that's it. And "you can use" is the action statement. "Use" is a verb. It implies work. And that's all on you, not me and not the book.

Remember, all I did was write this book to provide you with some information. You bought it with your own money, you read it and you made the decision to make the changes. I'm not going to steal your thunder by claiming I did anything but provide the information. My ego doesn't need to be stroked to the point where I'm going to take any credit like a lot of people who are saying they are changing lives, businesses and the world. My only role in all of this is to remind you that you have the ability to change your own life and give you a few tools to do it.

Mistakes? Big Deal

You're going to make mistakes. I promise you that you will. Lots of them. Often. Everybody screws up. I screw up all the time for sure. I could be the poster child for stupidity in life and business. I've made more mistakes than most people are ever going to make. I make more mistakes by noon than most people do in a whole month. It's because I'm busy and work hard. The percentages just work that way. When you are busy and doing a lot of stuff, then your chances that some of that stuff will be a mistake go up. I understand that and am good with it. That's the way I want you to be. I want you to make lots of mistakes because that's where the lessons are.

When you make mistakes, this is the process for dealing with them: First of all, admit it. Take responsibility for it. You're the one who screwed up. Take responsibility for screwing up and then go about the process of finding a solution.

One day, years ago, I was getting ready to walk out the door of my house heading to the airport to begin a series of speeches. My family is all standing around, including my son, who was nineteen years old at the time. He says, "Dad, I have yet to figure out why anybody would pay you to come and talk to them."

What a sweet thing for him to say, right? He says, "Dad, I've listened to your speech for years.

I've heard you tell people life is simple; business is simple. Dad, everything with you is always so simple. Dad, I live with you. That's not how you live your life. You've complicated life like everyone else. In fact, at this point, I don't think you have a clue about what it takes to be successful. I'm the one who has life figured out, not you."

"Well, son," I say, "obviously you have life figured out. You're nineteen years old. You just flunked out of your first semester of college, you just totaled your car and you just got fired. You're doing good!"

"Yeah, but I still know exactly what it takes to be successful."

"All right, if you're so smart, give it to me."

"All right, Dad, here it is. When you mess up, big deal. Just admit it, fix it, and move on. Other than that, life's a party."

You know what? He's right. Life really is just that simple. I've devoted all these pages to telling you what it takes to be successful in life, and my nineteen-year-old son summed it up in a sentence. When you mess up, big deal. Have you ever messed up? Of course, you have. Here's what I have to say about it: Big deal. You messed up.

Isn't that a cool way to look at things? What if you were just able to say, "Wow, I messed up. Big deal." Will you mess up again? You bet you will. You're always going to mess up. If you're not messing up, you're not doing anything. If you're ever going to do anything, you're going to mess up. And the more you do, the more you will mess up. Big deal.

That's about perspective. Mistakes are rarely fatal. Mistakes can be overcome. To expect to live a mistake-free life or run a mistake-free business is naïve. And it can't be done.

What my son said is the key to dealing with those mistakes. Number one: admit it. That's called taking responsibility. Most people on this planet never understand that concept. If that was all he ever learned from me then I was a pretty good daddy. Admit it, then fix it. Actually, most people are pretty good at this one. When they make a mess, most people are pretty good at cleaning their mess up. Very few people make a mess and leave it for somebody else. Some do for sure, but most people don't.

Admit it, fix it and move on. You have to learn to move past what you've done. I know there's that old saying that past behavior is the best predictor of future behavior. Yes, that's true. However, if you make a decision to change your future behavior regardless of your past behavior, you can do it.

Health and Happiness

Health and happiness are two things go hand in hand. It's really hard to be happy when you aren't healthy. And it's much harder to be healthy when you aren't happy. At least, that is my belief.

I have made a decision to be healthy. I have also made a decision to be happy. Every morning, I wake up and say to myself, "I am healthy, I am happy. I am rich." That is my affirmation. But, as the great Jim Rohn said, "Affirmation without implementation is self-delusion." The words I say don't mean much if I don't then do something to make those things happen. Otherwise, it's just pretty words. And we are a society who loves pretty words. We buy posters with pretty words on them. We buy books of quotes with pretty words. We listen to affirmation and meditations audios with pretty words. Give us pretty words and somehow we think everything will be okay. That's not how it works. Words are words. Words are powerful but still only words. Words need implementation to create results.

So, when I say to myself, "I am happy." I have to do what it takes to make sure I get that result. I have to back up the words with actions. When I say, "I am healthy." I have to back up those words with healthy actions. Saying I'm healthy won't do much for my health if I smoke two packs a day and eat fast food all day and do nothing but sit on my fat butt. They are still pretty words and a great affirmation but without proper action won't give me the desired result.

Same for my saying, "I am rich." If I said I am rich and then spent more than I earned, saying that I'm rich would be a lie.

Whatever you say, you have to be able to back it up with actions. If your decision is to be healthy then you need to do what healthy people do. And not spend so much time doing what unhealthy people do. Same for happy. What do happy people do? I can tell you for sure that they don't whine or wallow in their problems. Funny how many people claim they want to be happy yet do exactly that. They spend all of their time complaining about the things they have to be unhappy about. And, of course, it applies to rich as well. Rich people have rich actions to back up their words.

Wouldn't it make more sense to you to start doing as the people you want to be like? If you start doing what healthy people do, you end up healthy. If you start doing what rich people do, you end up rich. If you start doing what happy people do, you end up happy. If you start doing what successful people do, you end up successful. Simulate the actions of the people you want to be like.

Too many spend their time focusing on what they *don't* want to be and what they *don't* want to have happen. They focus on the results they don't want to have instead of the results they do want to have.

Healthy Hints

Let me give you a couple of quick ideas for being healthy and losing a little weight too. I'm no expert that's for sure but these are pretty simple and solid for a variety of reasons.

First of all, stop going to fast-food restaurants. At least not often. They make a living selling grease. I *love* grease. I want my last meal to be a chicken-fried steak with fried okra. And although I still indulge myself from time to time with a chicken-fried steak, I've learned you can't do that every single day.

Here's another idea. When you go someplace, park as far away as you possibly can without having to cross a major thoroughfare on foot. I don't want you getting run over on my suggestion! Park in the parking lot but far enough away to give yourself some distance to walk and get a little exercise. Take your dog for a walk. Take your kid for a walk. Go for a walk yourself. You don't really need a reason except to get off your fat butt and walk. Walking helps you lose weight. It's great exercise and you don't have to join a gym to do it. You just put on a pair of shoes and go for a walk. And if you live on a beach you don't even need the shoes.

Don't weigh yourself very often. When you weigh yourself every single day, you're going to get discouraged. Every other week or so, step up on the scale, and then figure out where you are. Don't be unrealistic. That's the problem. People expect they're going to lose five pounds a week. Chances are good that you didn't gain five pounds in a week, so you aren't going to lose five a week either.

Get a smaller plate. Yeah, I know, you've probably heard that before. And I used to laugh at this one. But it works. Smaller plate equals smaller portions. Smaller portions are good for you.

When you lose a little weight, reward yourself. Don't reward yourself with a bag of M&Ms or a piece of pie. That's a stupid reward that undermines your achievement. Instead, buy yourself something tight to wear. Pony up and buy something expensive. Buy it tight. Why? Because if you spend some money on it, you will be encouraged to keep losing weight until it will fit you with room to spare.

Splurge every once in a while. I like M&Ms. I mean, I *really* like M&Ms. There was a time in my life when I'd get a pound and a half of M&Ms, dump them all out on my desk, sort them by color, and eat them by color. Brown first just to get rid of them and green last. I like green M&Ms. I don't do that anymore because if you do that too often, you end up a fat boy. Now, I buy a little bitty package of M&Ms. Halloween size. I take a few out and I pour the rest into the toilet. Why do I pour them into the toilet? Because if I put them in the trash can, I'd go back and get them later on. And trust me, I would. If I just put the package in the trash, in an hour I would be digging in there to get them out. I'm not a believer in willpower. Willpower is overrated. I'm a believer in not making things available. I believe that we're only as strong as our options. I try to cut back on my options. So, I'll get a few M&Ms out to satisfy my sweet tooth and pour the rest of them down the toilet. Will a few make me happy? No, it won't make me happy, but it will satisfy an urge. It will be a very small indulgence.

It's okay to have small indulgences. I am not a believer in denial any more than I'm a believer in willpower. I can't deny myself things, so I've learned to indulge myself in very small ways periodically. Try it. It's much more realistic way to deal with eating than talking about all of the things you can't eat or shouldn't eat. Eat whatever you want only in smarter ways.

Drink lots of water. Always carry a bottle of water with you. First of all, none of us drink enough water. It flushes out your system, but it'll also fill you up. Hydrate!

Furthermore, stop blaming your weight on a condition. The truth is that most of the people in the world today, other than an incredibly small percentage, are overweight because they take in too many calories and don't burn enough calories. So, chances are that you don't have a glandular problem. The number of the people in this world who have a glandular problem is so small they don't even count in the obesity statistics. And don't ever tell people you're big-boned. You aren't big-boned. Your bones are pretty much the same size as everybody else's. Dinosaurs have big bones, not you.

I heard this one growing up, "My family is just heavy. We're heavy people." My family was heavy because they ate too much. Your family probably is heavy because they eat too much and sit around too much. Being overweight is not in your genes. Chances are you haven't been able to fit in your jeans for a good long while.

Stop Being a Spectator

We've become a nation of spectators. We're voyeuristic. We like to watch other people do what we aren't willing to do. We'd rather sit around watching people lose weight on television than to get off the couch and do what they're doing to lose weight. We would rather watch *Friends* on TV than be a friend or have a friend. We would rather watch people paint their living room on television than paint our own living room.

We want to watch people work. We don't want to work ourselves. That's one of the problems. Stop being a spectator in life. Stop watching other people live the life you want to live. Get off the couch. Turn off the television. Go live the life you enjoy watching others live.

Social media has made it even worse. "Look at my breakfast! Aren't those eggs beautiful?" "Oh my God, they are! Wish I had eggs like those." Okay, get up, go into your kitchen and cook some eggs.

All of this voyeurism serves to make us jealous and envious of the lives of others. We end up thinking that others are living a life we should be living when the truth is there life is about taking pictures and your life has become about looking at pictures. Who is actually living their life?

That jealousy and envy over how others live their lives leads to a sense of entitlement. We believe that we deserve to live the life of people we watch on television or see on Instagram. We don't want to do the work they might have done to live that way, but we still want the rewards. And then we get mad when we don't experience the same rewards. Jealously and envy lead to a sense of entitlement and that leads to meanness. Meanness leads to most of what we see on social media today. It's sad. It's sickening. Don't play that game.

Know what real living is. Get off the couch. Turn off the TV. Turn off your computer. Turn off your phone. Check out of social media for a while. Get out and live life instead of watching others live theirs.

What Really Causes Stress

Let's talk about one of people's biggest excuses for not being healthy, not being successful and not achieving what they want to achieve: Stress.

Stress is a popular topic. Turn on the television or go on social media and you will see people talking about stress. I know speakers who make a living doing stress management seminars. What a waste of time. Why do you want to learn to manage something you don't need or want? You don't need stress management. You don't need to go to a seminar. This is what you need to know about stress: Stress comes from knowing what is right and doing what is wrong.

Let's do an exercise. Right now, take a sheet of paper and write down the things you believe to be causing you stress. It might be the employee that works for you. It might be your spouse. It might be the fact that your kids are misbehaving. Maybe it's lack of money. Your job. Your health.

Now look at that list item by item. I'll guarantee you that you know exactly the right thing to do about every one of the things on your list. Don't argue with me. Regardless of what you wrote down, you know what you ought to do. In fact, you've probably known exactly what you ought to do for a good long while. The problem is you didn't do it.

It's not the thing on the list that is causing you the stress, it's the fact that you didn't do one thing about it. You didn't do what you know you should have done. You're causing the stress with your inactivity. Your stress is your own fault.

"I'm just so stressed. My boss causes me stress. That idiot in the cubicle next to me is causing me stress."

That's not true. Stop saying that. You're causing your own stress because you aren't willing to take action. You aren't willing to do the things you know you ought to do. Confront the idiot in the cubicle. I've already told you earlier in the book exactly how to do that. Or if your boss if costing you stress, either accept it, talk to them about it or quit and go get a different boss. I had a person write me just a few weeks ago complaining about their boss. It was a person who had written me four times in the past year about the same boss. Every time, they said they were losing their minds because of the stress. Every time, they asked me what they should do. Every time, I told them to accept it or quit. I told them that their boss probably wasn't going to change and that to keep complaining about the stress was ridiculous. I told them to take control of their life and quit and get another job. Every time, they responded by saying, "Really? Do you think I should?" This last time I told them to never write me again since they obviously valued the stress more than they did my advice.

Maybe you have a bad employee. Believe me, firing that employee is going to cause you a lot less stress than keeping them. You need to take action.

Maybe you know that you ought to lose weight. It's the knowledge that you need to lose weight and aren't doing anything about it that's causing you the stress, not the weight. Take action on what you know you need to do, and I promise you, you will get rid of the stress that's in your life.

This isn't complicated or hard. In fact, nothing about life is really all that hard. We make it hard. In fact, I firmly believe that we want it to be hard. And the reason we want it to be hard is that if we believe it's hard then we'll have an excuse for not doing well. There is no excuse for not doing well. Or at the bare minimum, for not doing a little better than you are right now.

The Three Reasons for Failure

There are three reasons people aren't successful: they're stupid, lazy, or they just don't give a damn. That's what it always comes down to.

How many people are really stupid? Although I've already pointed out that that we do stupid things, how many people are really stupid? Not many. Everybody pretty much always knows what they ought to do. Everybody at least knows one thing they could do to have more in their life, to be more successful, to have more money. Everybody knows that.

So, very few people are really stupid. It's not that we don't know. It's that we don't do what we know, which means we're lazy. People know what it takes to be successful and they're too lazy to do it. You know why? They don't give a damn. They don't care enough.

As I said, I don't care how you become rich. To become rich, you have to have a strong reason, a strong why. That's exactly what I'm talking about here. You have to care enough about success that you're willing to do whatever it takes. You have to know why you want to become successful. You have to know why you want to become wealthy. You have to know why you want to be healthy.

Why do you want to be healthy? Hopefully, so you can live a life that's full of everything that you want. So you can go to all the places you want to go. So you can do the things that you want to do. So you'll be around to enjoy your kids and grandkids. That's why you want to live a healthy life.

I do what I do because I know I can, and I want to push myself because it's fun and I enjoy the challenges. That is a motivator for me. I want to do things that no one in my family has ever done. I grew up dirt-poor. I wanted to be the first guy in my family to get a college degree. I wanted to be the first guy in my family to become a millionaire. I wanted to live in a house where, when you walk in the front door, you say, "Wow." I didn't do it to show off for others. I did it for me. I did it all to prove that I could. It was a way for me to measure my own success. I wanted to be healthy because I love my wife. I love my kids. I love my grand-kids. I love my two bulldogs. I want to be able to enjoy them, and in order to enjoy them, I have to be healthy.

Why are you doing what you do? Why is your life the way it is? Do you even care? If you're not doing the things that it takes to be successful in your life, why aren't you? Don't you care enough to do whatever it takes?

You probably already know what it takes to be successful. You have all along. If you didn't know, maybe I've given you some ideas in this little book. And if you're not successful and your life isn't where you want it to be or at least on the way to where you want it to be then it's because you either don't know (which I don't buy) or you're too lazy. And if that's the case then it's because you don't care.

I want that to change for you right now. I want you to start caring so much that you're not willing to accept anything but the very best for yourself and your life, and you can do it. If any one can do it then anyone can do it. Read that one again. If any one can do it then anyone can do it.

Short, Hard, Expensive Lessons

Let me finish with some short, hard, expensive lessons. These are one-sentence lessons. You don't need to spend a lot of time on them.

1. Do the right thing. Period. The right thing to do is rarely the easy thing to do but you need to do it anyway.

2. People will usually lie to protect themselves. Be aware of that.

3. Both companies and individuals overpromise and underdeliver. Knowing that in advance will save you time, money, and disappointment.

4. Everything costs more than you originally thought it would.

5. Everything takes longer than you originally thought it would.

6. When someone says, "I'm a people person," that means they'll spend more time socializing than working.

7. When someone says, "I don't like working with others," hire them. Give them an office with a door and a lot of work to do then watch it get done.

8. Prove you're smarter than everyone else by hiring people who are smarter than you are.

9. Don't expect others to make you rich if you're keeping them broke.

10. The more successful you become, the fewer friends you will have.

11. Take your job seriously, not yourself.

12. When someone says they will try to do it then you can bet your money it won't get done.

13. If you aren't willing to put your money where your mouth is, you don't really believe in what you're doing.

14. People will pay little attention to what you have to say. In fact, most won't even believe what you have to say. They will, however, pay attention to see if *you* believe what you have to say.

15. People motivate themselves. You have nothing to do with it.

16. Look at the numbers, look at the facts, then trust your gut.

17. Knowledge is not power. The implementation of knowledge is power.

18. Few people will take responsibility for their results until they have exhausted the opportunities to blame someone else.

19. Everybody does what they want to do when they want to do it and not until then.

20. The best advertisement in the whole world is a satisfied customer with a big mouth and the worst advertisement in the whole world is an unsatisfied customer with a big mouth.

21. Don't worry too much about making the right decision. Just make the decision, and then do what it takes to make the decision right.

22. You always need a plan B, except when you don't have one. In that case, you have to make your only plan work.

23. You can sell your way out of almost any problem.

24. Sometimes the best thing you can do is walk away.

25. Pay your taxes first, yourself second, and everyone else after that.

26. Trust, once destroyed, can never be fully regained.

27. If all of this starts to feel too complicated, stop, regroup, and start over. Success is always simple.

The Test for Success

At this point, you're probably saying, "If I do all of this stuff, Larry, will I be successful?" If you do all this, I believe you will be successful, but I have a test. I want you to take my little test for success, and if you answer yes to all of these questions, then I will consider you a success, and you ought to consider yourself a success. Here are the questions.

Am I happy?

Am I healthy?

Am I serving others?

Am I a loving person?

Am I constantly learning?

Am I having fun?

Am I doing something I enjoy?

Am I prosperous?

If you can answer yes to all those, celebrate. You're successful. That's what it really comes down to, and if you look at those questions, and you answered no, then you have to stop, and you have to do whatever it takes to turn those answers into a yes.

There you have it. You've read all these pages in which I tell you what it takes to be successful in business. I hope you will agree at this point that it's just not that hard. I promised you it would be simple, and it is. You don't need it to be hard. You need to remind yourself how simple it really is.

But let me warn you: you're going to get bogged down. You can't do everything that I've talked about here without getting bogged down. When it happens, and it will, and you'll feel disappointed, and you'll feel as if you're messing up. Just stop. Regroup. Start over again. Go back to the simple ideas. If you start to get ticked off and say, "Larry, this stuff doesn't work" then go to the mirror and say, "I created this mess. I created my problems. I have the ability to create my success." Talk to yourself a little. Be your own accountability coach.

When it starts feeling really complicated and you're bogged down, shake it off, put it in perspective, understand that success comes at a price and sometimes it's going to suck and get back after it.

When you're wondering about what it's going to take to fix your problem, it will always boil down to work. Never shortcut the work. Don't under-estimate work. It always comes down to work. Work hard on your job. Work hard at your tasks. Work hard on your plan. Work hardest on yourself.

CPSIA information can be obtained
at www.ICGtesting.com
Printed in the USA
JSHW031334220920
8144JS00007B/129